Brian Fleming Research & Learning Library
Ministry of Education
Ministry of Training, Colleges & Universities
900 Bay St. 13th Floor, Mowat Block
Toronto, ON M7A 1L2

SCHOOL DISTRICT LEADERSHIP MATTERS

STUDIES IN EDUCATIONAL LEADERSHIP

VOLUME 8

Series Editor
Kenneth Leithwood, OISE, University of Toronto, Canada

Editorial Board
Christopher Day, University of Nottingham, United Kingdom
Stephen Jacobson, Graduate School of Education, Buffalo, U.S.A.
Bill Mulford, University of Tasmania, Hobart, Australia
Peter Sleegers, University of Nijmegen, The Netherlands

SCOPE OF THE SERIES

Leadership we know makes all the difference in success or failures of organizations. This series will bring together in a highly readable way the most recent insights in successful leadership. Emphasis will be placed on research focused on pre-collegiate educational organizations. Volumes should address issues related to leadership at all levels of the educational system and be written in a style accessible to scholars, educational practitioners and policy makers throughout the world.

The volumes – monographs and edited volumes – should represent work from different parts in the world.

For further volumes:
http://www.springer.com/series/6543

SCHOOL DISTRICT LEADERSHIP MATTERS

by

BRUCE SHEPPARD

*Memorial University,
St. John's, NF, Canada*

JEAN BROWN

*Memorial University,
St. John's, NF, Canada*

and

DAVID DIBBON

*Memorial University,
St. John's, NF, Canada*

Dr. Bruce Sheppard
Memorial University
Fac. Education
Prince Philip Drive
St. John's NF A1B 3X8
Canada
bsheppar@mun.ca

Dr. Jean Brown
Memorial University
Fac. Education
Prince Philip Drive
St. John's NF A1B 3X8
Canada
jbrown@mun.ca

Dr. David Dibbon
Memorial University
Fac. Education
Prince Philip Drive
St. John's NF A1B 3X8
Canada
ddibbon@mun.ca

ISBN 978-1-4020-9746-1   e-ISBN 978-1-4020-9747-8

DOI 10.1007/978-1-4020-9747-8

Library of Congress Control Number: 2009920273

© Springer Science+Business Media B.V. 2009
No part of this work may be reproduced, stored in a retrieval system, or transmitted
in any form or by any means, electronic, mechanical, photocopying, microfilming, recording
or otherwise, without written permission from the Publisher, with the exception
of any material supplied specifically for the purpose of being entered
and executed on a computer system, for exclusive use by the purchaser of the work.

Printed on acid-free paper

9 8 7 6 5 4 3 2 1

springer.com

Preface

The ideas put forth in this book represent 25 years of research and practice with a particular emphasis on a reflective analysis of my (Sheppard's) efforts to lead meaningful change at the district level using available research evidence. My research and practice have been focussed on understanding how educational leaders in schools and school districts can bring about meaningful change with a moral purpose. My journey began during the 1980s, when I became the principal of a large high school. It was painfully obvious to me that classroom practices had remained essentially unchanged for decades, many students appeared not to be well served, and I wanted to make a difference. In that leadership role, I was constantly challenged and intrigued by the complexities of bringing about meaningful change. As I explored the literature on effective schools and change and attempted to apply the ideas to my leadership practices, it became readily apparent that some efforts were more beneficial than others. My thirst to better understand the leadership and change phenomenon led me to pursue advanced studies that marked the beginning of my academic career and has shaped my research agenda since then. However, for me, studying and writing about leadership for change was not enough. My goal of better understanding leadership in order to lead meaningful change drew me back to practice. Fortunately, I was given the opportunity to practice as a superintendent of education in a mid-size school district where my colleagues and I had been engaged in an action research project related to leadership, organizational learning, and changing practices to improve student learning. During those years, I maintained contact with my research colleagues, kept abreast of the emerging evidence related to educational leadership, and kept a reflective journal of my practice.

This book is not intended to give a historical account of successful district-level leadership. Even if I attempted to claim some success, my claim would be challenged, as I can think of no leader who has been "judged entirely successful, even those who have influenced millions" (Kouzes & Posner, 2003, p. 259). Reeves (2002) claims that a good guide for a book of this nature is as follows: "If you will learn from my mistakes, as well as the mistakes and successes I have observed in almost thirty years of leadership studies, everything will not necessarily be swell, but you will approach each challenge with greater insight and more confidence" (p. 115). It is to this purpose that this book is dedicated. Therefore, the intent of this book is to present the challenges, mistakes, successes, and new understandings developed as one leader attempted to employ the evolving leadership theory in order to bring about substantive district-level change with a moral purpose. Toward that end, my coauthors and I remained engaged as action researchers and critical friends throughout the entire duration of my practice as superintendent of education. During that period, I attempted to be a critical reflective practitioner who kept a detailed reflective journal of my journey as a superintendent. My coauthors in their role as academic researchers continued as critical friends to ensure the accuracy of my accounts and counteract my biases and uncovered beliefs through providing an in-depth critical analysis of my practice.

We are hopeful that our reflections upon and critical analysis of leadership practice that was intended to be grounded in current understandings of change theory, organizational learning, and emerging models of leadership that emphasize instructional, transformational, and value-based leadership will provide new insights and questions for academic researchers and will inspire policymakers and practitioners to imagine what might be and to work toward it. Furthermore, we hope that this book will assist senior-level practitioners as they wrestle with the application of theory to practice and that it will contribute to the advancement of our understanding of district-level leadership and how it interacts with leadership at the school and provincial levels in leading changes that impact student learning at the classroom level. Both practitioners and researchers should find this book of value.

References

Kouzes, J., & Posner, B. (2003). *Credibility*. San Francisco, CA: Jossey-Bass.
Reeves, D. (2002). *The daily disciplines of leadership*. San Francisco, CA: Jossey-Bass.

Acknowledgments

To the many individuals who contributed through participation in interviews or assisted in maintaining the archive of district documents that populated the superintendent's reflective journal and to those who will recognize themselves within the pages of this book, we thank you for your support to our research and for your commitment to the ongoing improvement of public education. In this regard, we extend a special note of appreciation to Gwen Hurley, executive assistant to the superintendent of Discovery School District, for her detailed record keeping that facilitated the retrieval of applicable district documents that were essential to the success of our research work that serves as the foundation of this book.

We thank the school board trustees of Discovery School District who were supportive of the district superintendent and who were willing to embark on the risky journey of shifting structures and engaging in decision-making processes that were facilitative of collaborative leadership and organizational learning. Similarly, we acknowledge and thank Discovery School District senior administrators, divisional directors, program specialists, school principals, and teachers for their openness to change and their willingness to engage in the facilitation of collaborative leadership throughout the school district. Without their collective support, there would have been little to write about.

We would like to specifically recognize Dr. Kenneth Leithwood, editor of this series, for his initial prompting to complete this work, for his encouragement and support throughout the process, and for his own research and writing that continue to shape our thinking related to school and district leadership.

Besides, we extend a note of appreciation to Will Oxford, Faculty of Education, Memorial University, for his proofreading of our final manuscript draft. Finally, we recognize Sarah (Sadie) Sheppard for the countless hours that she volunteered to proofread and edit the many drafts of each chapter that compose this book. Without her work and continued support and encouragement, this book may never have been completed.

Contents

1 Where Theory Meets Practice 1
   Our Case Study Methodology 3
   The District Case 5
   The Sociopolitical Context of Discovery School District 8
   Charting a New Course 10
   References 12

2 Leadership and Organizational Learning 15
   Confronting the Challenge 18
   How Can Formal Leaders Facilitate Collaborative Leadership and
   Organizational Learning? 20
      Study One 20
      Study Two 21
      Study Three 23
      Study Four 24
      Study Five 25
   Implications for the Implementation and Practice of Collaborative
   Leadership 26
   References 29

3 Meeting the Challenges of Hierarchy Through District Leadership 33
   Overcoming Resistance to Collaborative Leadership Through District
   Leadership 34
   My Voice 39
   Through the Lens of Critical Friends 43
   References 45

4 Establishing Collaborative Structures 49
   My Voice 52
      Nurturing Collaborative Leadership at Discovery School District 52
      Collaboratively Defining Shared Decision-Making 57
   Through the Lens of Critical Friends 61

        Analysis of the Structural Changes 61
        Teacher Perceptions of Collaboration 63
    Conclusion 65
    References 66

5 Strategic Thinking and Adaptive Learning 69
    My Voice 72
        Strategic Planning in Discovery School District 72
        Developing a Shared Vision for Teaching and Learning 78
        Personal Reflections 80
        A Final Observation 80
    Through the Lens of Critical Friends 81
    References 83

6 Professional Development and Capacity Building 85
    Professional Development in Discovery School District 88
    My Voice 91
        Adopting a New Approach to Professional Development 92
    Through the Lens of Critical Friends 96
    References 99

7 Systems Challenges to Growth and Sustainability of Meaningful Educational Reform 101
    Toward Meaningful School Reform 102
    Systems Thinking in Discovery School District 105
    Systems Challenges to the Discovery School District Reform Agenda 106
        Challenge 1: Government Control of Financial and Human Resources ... 106
        Challenge 2: The Difficult Transition from Purpose to Practice 109
        Challenge 3: Localized Education in a Globalized World 110
        Challenge 4: A Market-Oriented Approach to School District
        Restructuring 113
    References 117

8 Recognizing What Makes Effective School Districts 121
    Recognitions: Discussion, Implications, and Recommendations 124
    Final Thoughts 131
    References 132

About the Authors 135

Author Index 137

Subject Index 141

Chapter 1
Where Theory Meets Practice

Abstract Confidence in public education has declined over the last few decades with the accumulated effect of increased centralized authoritarian control of the education system by governments. This trend of increased government control appears to run counter to the existing empirical evidence that highlights the importance of collaborative leadership that is facilitative of organizational learning as a means of bringing about successful change and improved student learning. Unfortunately, the literature related to collaborative leadership has suffered from a lack of specificity that is needed to guide the actual practices of district superintendents who are responsible for the administration and leadership of very complex organizations that for the most part continue to be bureaucratic hierarchies. It was with the objective of contributing to the needed evidence that we engaged in our district study and have written this book.

Barth (1990) compared the life of an adult working in a school to a tennis shoe in a laundry dryer. Having been a teacher, a principal, and an assistant superintendent in the k-12 school system and having escaped Barth's laundry dryer, I (Sheppard) had the opportunity to research, study, and reflect upon the practice that I had loved, but with which I had been frustrated because of the system's intransigence to change. As a practitioner, I had been frustrated by academics, politicians, and senior administrators who believed that they had all the answers and that the problem with education was that teachers were just unwilling to follow their edicts. On the other hand, as an academic, I found that while there existed much rhetoric among practitioners around collaborative leadership and organizational learning[1], they were often no more than the current "buzzwords" or just another nice partnership project to be pursued (Sheppard, 2003; Sheppard & Brown, 1999, 2000a, 2000b, 2000c). As a result, I was often drawn to think, "If I had been aware of this when I was a

---

[1] We employ the term *organizational learning* somewhat synonymously with professional learning communities and learning organizations, with both of the latter terms referring to organizations or communities of practice, such as schools and school boards, which are engaged in organizational learning.

school principal, I would have ...." "Why doesn't that superintendent[2] of education realize ...?" "If I were superintendent I would work to facilitate more collaborative leadership and organizational learning."

Then one day, I was face-to-face with the prospect of becoming the superintendent of a district where I had been involved as a "critical friend" and action researcher focused on the development of schools and the school district as learning organizations. My passion for practice got the better of me, and I headed back to the school system once again. I thought, surely, as superintendent, I can really lead the creation of a professional learning community that will make a real difference to student learning.

Having been superintendent for five years and having once again returned to the relative calm of an academic environment, I can truly say that Barth's metaphor of the tennis shoe in the laundry dryer captures not only adults at the school level, but the experiences of senior administrators at the school district level as well. School consolidation, legal challenges, law suits, employee grievances, government control, turf protection, budget deficits, government fiscal constraints, infrastructure problems, student suspensions, student transportation issues, public scrutiny, the media hunger for sensationalism, and other administrative routines often diverted attention from the student learning agenda. From my vantage point as superintendent, I became very aware of the applicability and accuracy of the following observation by Barth (1990), not only for schools, but also for school districts:

> Research frequently provides a broad view, badly needed in schools. Yet, the data base is, in many respects, thin. Researchers pay brief visits to many schools, asking few questions of a large sample, frequently with all the effects of a tea bag swished through a bathtub. (p. 150)

Besides, Chester Barnard's (1964) observation of many decades ago became very real to me. None of the literature of which I was aware described school districts or school district leadership

> in a way which seemed to me to correspond either to my experience or to understanding implicit in the conduct of those recognized to be adept in executive practice or in leadership of organizations .... Always, it seemed to me, the scientists—from whatever side they approached—just reached the edge of organization as I experienced it, and retreated .... But the bridge between the generalizations of social study on the one hand and the action of the masses of which they related on the other were not included, I thought. (Barnard, 1964, p. viii–ix)

Barnard's claim was that "It is in this field that for thirty years I have had intimate and continuous experience. Those who possess the general knowledge and the scientific training required usually do not have such experience" (Barnard, 1964, p. xii). Believing that there is merit in Barnard's aforementioned perspective, I feel that a particular strength of this work is my unique combination of academic empirical research and practice. The level of intimacy with the application of the theory to practice that I bring to this work is rare, and it brings insights that can only be

---

[2] We employ the term *superintendent* to refer to the most senior administrative position (chief executive officer) in a school district.

provided by the precise four-stage cycle of my administrative career: (1) practical leadership experience, (2) academic reflection, (3) practical leadership experience, and (4) academic reflection. "To avoid the inherent bias in the historical accounts of those who win the battle" (Reeves, 2002, p. 115), I combine my insights with those of two co-authors who as researchers and critical friends challenged both my leadership practice as superintendent and my reflective analysis of that experience. As a consequence, consistent with Reeves' suggestion, what we offer in this work is "no victor's history"; rather, we "share warts and all" (p. 115).

Our Case Study Methodology

Prior to my assuming the position of superintendent, Brown and I had been involved with the case study district as "critical friends" and action researchers focused on the facilitation of organizational learning in 11 selected schools. Our action research project was initiated by a district program specialist and supported by senior district administrators, including the superintendent. During year one, we visited each of the school sites, at which time we conducted introductory information sessions in respect to the empirical evidence related to collaborative leadership and organizational learning and our role as critical friends and action researchers. During the spring of year one, we collected survey data of teachers' perceptions of leadership and organizational learning at their respective schools and throughout the school district. During the fall of year two, we presented the individual school-level findings to the entire staff of each participating school. After having completed all school-level presentations, during early winter we shared the specific district-level findings and aggregated school-level data with the senior administrative team of the district. In the spring of the second year, I accepted a five-year contract as superintendent in our case school district, and Dibbon joined Brown to replace me as the second member of the external research team. While I could not continue as an external researcher, as superintendent I would remain a member of the action research team as a practitioner. I would apply theory to practice as a means of facilitating the development of a more collaborative leadership approach directed at fostering district-wide organizational learning, while Brown and Dibbon would continue as critical friends and researchers. From a research perspective, we considered that the circumstance created by my having assumed the role of superintendent of Discovery School District with a commitment to the application of collaborative leadership and organizational learning theory to practice would provide an excellent *deviant case sample* (Martella, Nelson, & Marchand-Martella, 1999).

Prior to accepting the position of superintendent, I informed the school board of my intended approach to leadership that would be empirically driven, collaborative, and rooted in respect for people. For instance, in my opening presentation to the school board, I stated,

> It is my commitment that I will be guided by ... a philosophy of leadership that is rooted in respect for people. I will operate from the principle that the leadership provided in this

district must be collaborative and very much dependent upon the collective wisdom of students, school and district staff and administrators, trustees, schools councils and other educational stakeholders. (Board Meeting minutes, May 24, 2000)

Our approach to action research was consistent with that proposed by Greenwood and Levin (2000) as a means of developing a closer relationship between theory and praxis in the social sciences. They define action research as "research in which the validity and value of research results are tested through collaborative insider-professional research knowledge generation and application processes" (p. 94). Our use of the term critical friend is consistent with the following description by Costa and Kallick (1993):

> A trusted person who asks provocative questions, provides data to be examined through another lens, and offers critique of a person's work as a friend. A critical friend takes the time to fully understand the context of the work presented and the outcomes that the person or group is working toward. The friend is an advocate for the success of that work. (p. 50)

Through this process, all three of us worked together frequently to explore and challenge our understandings of the research literature. We collected qualitative data over a five-year period as both participants-as-observers and observers-as-participants (Martella et al., 1999). The critical research friends kept careful field notes when they attended district meetings and conducted professional development sessions within the district. As superintendent, I kept a journal that included detailed notes and links to important records and documents (e.g., keynote addresses and presentation notes, policy papers, and meeting minutes) that I shared with my critical research colleagues. In regular meetings, we analyzed what was happening, asked and answered questions, and explored the challenges of linking theory to practice and the emerging trends.

At the end of the five-year period, and after having analyzed data from my reflective journal and compared it to the analysis of data from observations and other information sources, my critical friends conducted in-depth interviews with me, during which time they challenged journal entries and the perspectives expressed in order to uncover hidden biases. Notes from those interviews provided an additional source of data. Other data sources included interviews with key informants including school board trustees, assistant superintendents, and other district-level professionals; newspaper clippings; documents used at in-service sessions; policy documents; and organizational charts and diagrams.

Our qualitative data analysis was grounded in the collaborative leadership and organizational learning framework (see Chapter 2 for a detailed description of this framework). We organized the district data into one large data file that we studied independently to identify and assess the extent to which the processes, structures, and procedures were consistent with our articulation of a collaborative approach to leadership and organizational learning. Employing procedures as outlined by LeCompte and Preissle (1993), we reviewed all the data and documentation that we had collected. We looked for completeness and sought additional information when we discovered gaps in our knowledge. We worked independently and then collaboratively as we made sense of the data. We assembled chunks of the data and summarized them in narrative form and linked together major events and issues. We then prioritized the themes, establishing what was of the greatest significance in our analysis of the organizational learning conditions and in answering our research question of how a school district superintendent can influence each of those conditions by employing a collaborative approach to leadership that was informed by the emerging empirical evidence. Further, we attempted to determine if and how leadership approach and organizational learning facilitated improvements in teaching and learning throughout both the school and district levels.

Additionally, we collected data related to leadership approach and organizational learning conditions through teacher surveys.[3] We had previously employed these survey instruments (Sheppard & Brown, 1999) and had found that the internal consistency reliability coefficients (Cronbach Alpha) for each of the scales ranged from 0.788 to 0.900. As noted above, we administered these surveys several months prior to the superintendent succession and again approximately four years later. For the initial administration of the surveys, school participation was voluntary (11 schools and 215 teachers). During the second administration of the surveys, all schools participated (32 schools and 606 teachers). Return rates in our participating schools were in excess of 86% for both Survey One and Survey Two.

For our comparative analysis of changes from Survey One to Survey Two, we focused only on the original 11 schools in order to assess changes in the original schools and to maintain relatively equal sample sizes: 215 for Survey One and 237 for Survey Two. To test our null hypothesis that there were no statistically significant differences between Year One and Year Four results, we employed analysis of variance (or the Welch statistic in cases when the assumption of equal variance did not hold). We calculated effect sizes (Cohen's d) using pooled standard deviations.

To maximize the reliability and validity of our analysis, we were guided by the standards set by Franklin and Jordan (1995): "completeness of information; adequacy of interpretation; determination of inconsistencies in data; adequacy of metaphors, pictures, or diagrams; collaboration with participants; and multiple methods to gather data." In case of multiple methods, for example, we strengthened the reliability and validity of our data through data source and methods triangulation (Martella et al., 1999) by using a variety of data collection methods and sources while employing both quantitative and qualitative approaches.

The District Case

Discovery School District (a pseudonym) is a rural school district with approximately 11,000 students that had existed for only one year prior to the initiation of the action research project that forms the foundation of this district case study. The district was created as a result of a provincial government school board reform

---

[3] The survey instrument is a modified version of the *Sources and Nature of Leadership and Process of Professional Learning Survey* (Leithwood, 1995a, 1995b).

initiative whereby four previous boards that had been religious-based were collapsed into one public school board in order to reduce expenditures and improve efficiencies. The mandate of the newly created public school board was to eliminate any excess school building capacity that had resulted from denominational education and declining student populations. This required the board and district-level administrators to focus on the difficult challenge of school consolidation and school closures that had the potential to divert attention away from student learning.

Student academic performance in Discovery School District was on par with that of other school districts in the province on provincial measures that included criterion reference tests at grades 3, 6, and 9 and public examinations at the high-school level. However, provincial achievement levels were lower than the national average in national and international achievement tests such as the School Achievement Indicators Program (SAIP), Programme for International Student Assessment (PISA), and Trends in Mathematics and Science Achievement around the World (TIMSS). In response to this reality, the provincial department of education pressured all school boards to place an increased emphasis on improving student performance on all of those tests that primarily focused on mathematics, science, and language arts. Discovery School District, similar to other districts, responded to the provincial pressure and set specific plans to improve test scores. As a result of the increased focus on improving test scores, a growing number of school and district personnel raised concerns that subject areas that were not tested such as the visual and performing arts and physical education had been allowed to languish within the district. It appears that *what was measured was valued!*

In spite of the district-level leaders' articulation of a focus on the improvement of student test scores, our analysis of the baseline data collected during the first year revealed that teachers were generally unaware of any district-wide initiative focused on improving student learning. While 81% of the teachers answering our survey indicated that they thought that developing a vision for the school was important, only 36% perceived that they had a school vision that guided their actions. It is also noteworthy that only 64% of the teachers surveyed believed that collaborative activities at their school were focused on student learning even though 94% of them believed that planning for and helping students was their most important work.

In respect to the perceived leadership approach, survey results indicated that the majority of pilot schools, at least, were functioning as traditional hierarchical organizations. Fewer than 70% of teachers in the pilot schools perceived the principal as democratic, participatory, or inclusive (see Table 1.1); and just over 60% perceived that the principal was a source of leadership, and this was the highest rating of all groups (see Table 1.2). In contrast, in a previous study of a school (Vision Collegiate) in another district that had been recognized as an innovative school (Sheppard & Brown, 2000a), 100% of the staff saw the principal as a key source of leadership (see Table 1.2), and over 90% saw her/him as democratic, participatory, or inclusive (see Table 1.1). In this latter school, the ratings given for the leadership provided by other groups were consistently higher than any (including the principal) in our pilot schools. As for teachers' perceptions of leadership provided by

Table 1.1 Teachers' perceptions of principal's leadership approach

Approach	District (%)	Vision Collegiate (%)
Democratic	70	97
Participatory	69	100
Inclusive	61	93

Table 1.2 Teachers' perceptions of sources of leadership within school

Source	District (%)	Vision Collegiate (%)
Principal	63	100
Vice principal	55	90
Department heads	33	73
Teachers assigned a role	55	87
Team of principal and vice principal	56	90

Table 1.3 Teachers' perceptions of external sources of leadership

Source	District (%)	Vision Collegiate (%)
School board members	10	7
Superintendent	15	17
Assistant superintendents	11	13
Program specialists	24	20
District-wide committee	8	13
Parents/community	23	27
Department of education	6	3

district-level personnel, the ratings were quite low in both Vision Collegiate and the pilot schools in Discovery School District (see Table 1.3). In the pilot schools, for instance, 24% of teachers perceived that program specialists[4] provided leadership support. This was the highest rating given to any district-level group. In fact, teachers perceived that parents and the community provided more leadership support (23%) than did the school board (10%) or school district administrators (11–15%).

Our analysis of district organizational charts and of meeting minutes of the existing organizational structures and our interviews with assistant superintendents revealed that the school district was a typical bureaucratic hierarchy, thereby mirroring the most common administrative structures and practices found in other school districts (Bimber, 1994; Green, 2001). The administrative structures included Administrative Council (the superintendent and assistant superintendents), General Advisory Council (selected representatives of program specialists and school principals), Program Specialists' Meetings, and Principals' Meetings (principals, program specialists, and Administrative Council). The only administrative structure with decision-making authority was the Administrative Council where the model of

---

[4] Professional educators whose defined role was to provide program and professional development support to teachers. These professionals are referred to as program coordinators or staff development officers in other jurisdictions.

decision-making was one of debate with final decisions made by the superintendent. The General Advisory Council was constituted to provide advice to the superintendent. Program Specialists' Meetings, chaired by the assistant superintendent of programs, were held biweekly. In these meetings, program specialists made decisions related to teacher professional development and the implementation of new programs; however, decisions made in those meetings were subject to being overruled by the Administrative Council. The model of decision-making employed at Program Specialists' Meetings, similar to that employed at Administrative Council Meetings, was hierarchical, with the assistant superintendent of programs having the final say. Besides, most of the decisions that were made at all of those above-noted district-level meetings impacted constituents at the school-level without their having any input into the decision-making process. Principals' Meetings occurred approximately four times a year for the purpose of administrative updates and dissemination of materials from district-level personnel. Principals and other school-level constituents had no formal role in decision-making for the district. In fact, there existed no structure that supported participatory leadership or collaborative decision-making at the district level. Interviews with each of the assistant superintendents, the outgoing superintendent, and the superintendent's executive assistant revealed that the model of leadership within the district was predominantly hierarchically organized by rank and authority.

The Sociopolitical Context of Discovery School District

In recent years, public school systems have been portrayed as troubled organizations. This has made them favored targets for politicians whose mantra has been that they will improve the school system by legislating higher standards and increasing the accountability of educators to meet those standards (Hargreaves & Fink, 2006; Schlechty, 2005; Starratt, 2004). Irrespective of the legitimacy of the claim that the public school system is underperforming or the wisdom of governments' exerting more authoritarian control over the education system in attempts to improve it (Barlow & Robertson, 1994; Giles & Hargreaves, 2006; Goodlad, 2001; Starratt, 2004), the accumulating effect of both has been a growing loss of public confidence in our school system and an increased pressure on educational leaders (Fullan, 2000; Mulford, Silins, & Leithwood, 2004; Schlechty, 2005; Starratt, 2004). Mulford et al. observe, for instance, that "the external world of the educational leader is one of increasing loss of control as education systems in many countries have tightened centralized control mechanisms through accountability devices such as high [stakes] testing, performance management and competency frameworks" (p. 1). Similarly, Schlechty (2005) opines that those committed to public education feel embattled as they hear on "nearly every front ... how poorly the schools are doing" (p. 213).

Ironically, the accumulative effect of this loss of public confidence is increased support for and the implementation of even more centralized authoritarian control of our education system by governments, resulting in an increasing erosion of educational leaders' and teachers' autonomy (Schlechty, 2001). The most likely consequence of the continued disenfranchisement of educators from school reform is a continued downward spiraling of public confidence in public education (Littky, 2004; Popham, 2004; Shaker & Grimmett, 2004). In reality, few would argue that schools do not need to change or improve. For instance, Elmore (2002) argues that the most significant elements of today's schools remain the same as they have been over the last 100 years. Teachers still operate in isolation from one another, and they are expected to deliver content to students. Moreover, he contends that "the existing structure in the culture of schools seem better designed to resist learning and improvement than to enable it" (p. 4). Starratt (2004) holds a similar dim view of the performance of public schools stating that "despite sincere efforts of many [school personnel], the schooling process remains a huge waste of students' time and taxpayers' money" (p. 2). Similarly, Schlechty (2001) opines that schools have not kept pace with our changing social context. Even though we have shifted "from a society in which only the culturally elite and intellectually gifted were expected to achieve at high levels of academic competence to a society in which nearly all students are expected to perform at levels once assumed to be the purview of a few" (Schlechty, 2001, p. 10), "schools are not much different . . . than they were fifty years ago" (p. xi). Glickman, Gordon, & Ross-Gordon (2007) concur that school reform is necessary; however, they highlight the growing empirical evidence that "we cannot improve education by simply legislating higher standards and higher stakes" (p. 30). They contend that in order to bring about meaningful reform of our schools, the norms of the one-room schoolhouse that include "isolation, psychological dilemma, routine, inadequate teacher induction, inverted beginner responsibilities, lack of career stages, and absence of shared technical culture" (p. 32) must be challenged.

While we share the view that schools and school systems need to be more relevant in respect to meeting the learning needs of students in the twenty-first century, we are convinced that there are at least two significant challenges that impede the ability of schools and school systems to make the necessary changes. The first of these challenges, as discussed above, relates to the large number of change efforts that have been imposed by external sources. "Instead of [educational] organizations having the autonomy to consider, plan, and launch their own change initiatives, over the last several decades external forces such as [governments] and . . . policymakers, the courts, and various experts have set the change agenda" (Hall & Hord, 2006, p. 1). In this respect, Fullan's (1993) observation of over a decade ago appears to be relevant today: "The main problem in public education is not resistance to change, but the presence of too many innovations mandated or adopted uncritically and superficially on an ad hoc fragmented basis" (p. 23).

A second challenge is that student learning is impacted by multiple factors, many of which appear to be outside the direct control of educators (Kohn, 2002; Leithwood, Louis, Anderson, & Wahlstrom, 2004; Stoll & Fink, 1996; Wang & Walberg, 1991). For instance, Wang and Walberg identified 228 variables in their synthesis of the evidence from research and expert opinion in respect to variables that impact student learning and classified them into six broad categories: implementation, classroom instruction, and climate; program design; student variables; school-level variables; out-of-school context; and state/province and district variables. Just a quick glance at these categories reveals that much remains outside of the direct control of public school personnel. For instance, they cannot decide the type of student who will be enrolled in their school; they have little influence on the out-of-school context (e.g., socioeconomic conditions and the extent to which education is valued in the community); and school and classroom conditions such as class size, teacher workload, program design, and implementation decisions are typically controlled by the state/province and/or the school district. Stoll and Fink (1996) highlight the magnitude of challenge for schools as they observe that only "between 8% and 14% of the total variance in pupils' achievement is attributable to school" (p. 37). Obviously, expectations that school personnel alone can effectively deal with such complex, systemic challenges are unrealistic and naïve.

Charting a New Course

In recognition of the systemic nature of the multiple factors that inhibit or facilitate school improvement, and with increased understanding that solutions cannot be imposed by legislators or found in our schools alone, there has been a growing body of empirical evidence that has fueled support for the importance of organizational learning as a promising vision for bringing about meaningful school reform (Dufour, 2004; Fullan, 2005; Giles & Hargreaves, 2006; Hall & Hord, 2006; Leithwood et al., 2004). As it applies to schools and school systems, the term *organizational learning* refers to the professional, organizational, and leadership capacity and processes within a school or school district to maintain and improve organizational performance based on experience and collaborative learning with the intent of improving student learning.

Argyris (1999) contends that only organizations that have a capacity to learn are able to deal successfully with the uncertainties and ambiguities that occur naturally throughout the change process. If one accepts Argyris's claim, the relevance of organizational learning for schools is evident. Few would contest a claim that schools qualify as organizations facing a great deal of uncertainty and that there is a societal expectation that schools and classrooms undergo major change. While much of the research related to organizational learning has been conducted in non-school environments, there has been a growing number of researchers who support the claim that organizational learning offers considerable promise for educational reform (Dibbon, 2000; Fullan, 2005; Giles & Hargreaves, 2006; Hall & Hord, 2006; Leithwood et al., 2004; Louis, 2007; Sheppard, 2008; Sheppard & Brown, 2007). For example, Hall and Hord (2006) view organizational learning as the best hope for bringing about successful school improvement:

> We have observed and studied a few schools that have the cultural attributes of a learning organization; and we profoundly believe that schools must develop this kind of context if real and continuous change and improvement are to occur. (Hall & Hord, 2006, p. 35)

Further, they contend that

> Change success depends less on whether the source of change is internal or external and significantly more on the degree to which the culture of the organization is open and ready to consider what is currently being done and is continually examining ways to improve. The ideal condition is to have a professional learning community. (p. 1)

While we share the optimism related to the potential of organizational learning (now more commonly referred to as professional learning community in schools and school districts), we have observed that similar to previous terms used to describe efforts to improve schools (e.g., effective schools movement), the professional learning community framework is currently threatened. The term *professional learning community* has been co-opted by schools, school districts, departments of education, and consulting firms as the current label of choice (the buzzword of the day) without any consideration of its theoretical underpinnings or the growing empirical evidence base. Simplistic recipes that offer immediate transformation of a school into a professional learning community continue to proliferate, and in some jurisdictions, all schools have been renamed as professional learning communities. Having already observed such simplistic approaches, Louis (2007) opined that "A shift in a typical school's culture toward a PLC (professional learning community) will not occur through a year-long principal initiated work plan" (p. 5). Similar observations have led Hall and Hord (2006) to ponder if it is becoming a fad or "innovation du jour" (p. 270) as they observe that many schools announce that they are professional learning communities without having any of the attributes or characteristics that have been identified as most valued in professional learning communities. Dufour (2004) raises a similar concern as he observes that "the term has been used so ubiquitously that it is in danger of losing all meaning" (p. 6). It appears that although the *professional learning community* terminology has become common parlance in our schools, the reliability of reports of its widespread existence, at least with any degree of fidelity, is as rare as a sighting of the Loch Ness Monster.

In reality, organizational learning is a complex innovation that represents a dramatic departure from the traditional bureaucratic hierarchical framework that has become the accepted norm. Consequently, it must itself be implemented, and that implementation is an inherently complex process (Hall & Hord, 2006). While we may know what to do, it is not so easy to do it! While we agree with Louis (2007) that developing schools and school systems as professional learning communities needs "a culture change that will require years" (p. 5) to accomplish, unlike Louis who argues that the development of a professional learning community is not an innovation to be implemented, we contend that such a culture change will not occur without deliberate implementation of professional learning communities as a complex innovation and this is unlikely to occur without strong leadership. Schein (1992) warns that if leaders don't manage culture, it will "manage them" (p. 15). In our view, the shift that is required falls within what Hall and Hord (2006) refer to as a "large scale innovation that require[s] major changes in the roles of teachers, principals, and schools [and] take[s] five to eight years to implement" (p. 8). And "administrative leadership is essential to long-term change successes" (p. 10).

The importance of formal leadership has been identified as crucial to the change process and to improving student learning in studies related to leadership (Leithwood et al., 2004), effective schools (Edmonds, 1979; Elmore, 2000; Gezi, 1990), school improvement (Crandall, 1983; Hallinger & McCary, 1990; Louis & Miles, 1990), and school change and implementation (Fullan, 2005, 1999, 1993; Hall & Hord 2006; McLaughlin, 1990). In spite of the voluminous evidence of the importance of leadership, there remains a lack of clarity related to essential elements of successful leadership in schools and even less so in school districts. There is even less specificity in respect to how the theories related to collaborative leadership and organizational learning might guide the actual practices of a district superintendent who is responsible for the administration and leadership of a very complex organization (Murphy & Hallinger 2001; McLaughlin & Talbert 2003; Spillane, 1996). Fullan (2005) observes that the practice of successful leadership is very difficult as he opines that "it has always been hard enough for individuals to be good at theory or good at practice" (p. 104) and successful leaders must be both theoreticians and practitioners at the same time. It is our view that this presents a huge challenge that is unlikely to be overcome without the development of better, more precise images of these emerging empirically based leadership and organizational theories in practice.

In the remaining chapters of this book, we take a micro look at such leadership. We explore in detail the actions and reflections of one theoretician superintendent in Discovery School District who attempted over a five-year period to employ the available evidence and theoretical frameworks related to collaborative leadership and organizational learning directed at improving student learning. While it is not our intent to claim that there is *one best way*, we believe that the rich insights that we have gained through our in-depth analysis of leadership practices that were (or were intended to be) grounded in the current empirical and theoretical literature should advance our theoretical understandings and provide rich images of the practical application of these emerging empirically based theories related to educational leadership and organizational learning at the school district level.

References

Argyris, C. (1999). *On organizational learning*. Malden, MA: Blackwell.
Barlow, M. & Robertson, H. (1994). *Class warfare: The assault on Canada's schools*. Toronto: Key Porter Books.
Barnard, C. (1964). *The functions of the executive*. Cambridge, MA: Harvard University Press.
Barth, R. (1990). *Improving schools from within*. San Francisco, CA: Jossey-Bass.
Bimber, B. (1994). *The decentralizing mirage: Comparing decision-making arrangements in four high schools* (MR-459-GGF-LE). Santa Monica, CA: RAND. Retrieved from http://www.rand.org/pubs/online/education/index.html
Costa, A., & Kallick, B. (1993). Through the lens of a critical friend. *Educational Leadership, 51*(2), 49–51.
Crandall, D. (1983). The teacher's role in school improvement. *Educational Leadership, 41*(3), 6–9.
Dibbon, D. C. (2000). Diagnosing the extent of organizational learning in schools. In K. Leithwood (Ed.), *Understanding schools as intelligent systems* (pp. 211–236). Stanford, CT: JAI Press.

References

Dufour, R. (2004). Leadership is an affair of the heart. *Journal of Staff Development, 25*(1), 67–68.

Edmonds, R. (1979). Some schools work and more can. *Social Policy, 9*(5), 28–32.

Elmore, R. (2000). *Building a new structure for school leadership*. Washington, DC: The Albert Shanker Institute.

Elmore, R. (2002). *Bridging the gap between standards and achievement: The imperative for professional development in education*. Washington, DC: The Albert Shanker Institute.

Franklin, C., & Jordan, C. (1995). Qualitative assessment: A methodological review. *Families in Society, 76*, 281–295.

Fullan, M. (1993). *Change forces: Probing the depths of educational reform*. New York: The Falmer Press.

Fullan, M. (1999). *Change forces: The sequel*. New York: The Falmer Press.

Fullan, M. (2000). Introduction. In M. Fullan (Ed.), *The Jossey-Bass reader on educational leadership* (pp. xix–xxi). San Francisco, CA: Jossey-Bass.

Fullan, M. (2005). *Leadership and sustainability*. Thousand Oaks, CA: Corwin Press.

Gezi, K. (1990). The role of leadership in inner-city schools. *Educational Research Quarterly, 12*(4), 4–11.

Giles, C., & Hargreaves, A. (2006). The sustainability of innovative schools as learning organizations and professional learning communities during standardized reform. *Educational Administration Quarterly, 42*(1), 124–156.

Glickman, C., Gordon, S., & Ross-Gordon, J. (2007). *SuperVision and instructional leadership: A developmental approach*. Needham Heights, MA: Allyn & Bacon.

Goodlad, J. (2001). Convergence. In R. Soder, J. Goodlad, & T. McMannon (Eds.), *Developing democratic character in the young* (pp. 1–25). San Francisco, CA: Jossey-Bass.

Green, R. (2001). New paradigms in school relationships: Collaborating to enhance student achievement. *Education, 121*(4), 737.

Greenwood, D. J., & Levin, M. (2000). Reconstructing the relationships between universities and society through action research. In N. K. Denzin & Y. S. Lincoln (Eds.), *Handbook of qualitative research* (2nd ed., pp. 85–106). Thousand Oaks: Sage.

Hall, G., & Hord, S. (2006). *Implementing change: Patterns, principles, and potholes*. Toronto: Pearson Education.

Hallinger, P., & McCary, C. (1990). Developing the strategic thinking of instructional leaders. *The Elementary School Journal, 91*(2), 89–107.

Hargreaves, A., & Fink, D. (2006). *Sustainable leadership*. San Francisco, CA: Jossey-Bass.

Kohn, A. (2002). Fighting the tests: A practical guide to rescuing our schools. *Our Schools Our Selves, 11*(3), 85–114.

LeCompte, M. D. & Preissle, J. (1993). *Ethnography and qualitative design in educational research* (2nd ed.). San Diego: Academic Press.

Leithwood, K. (1995a). *The sources and nature of leadership: Staff survey*. Toronto: OISE.

Leithwood, K. (1995b). *The process of professional learning: Staff survey*. Toronto: OISE.

Leithwood, K., Louis, K., Anderson, S., & Wahlstrom, K. (2004). *How leadership influences student learning*. Retrieved Nov. 28, 2005 from http://www.wallacefoundation.org/WF/KnowledgeCenter/KnowledgeTopics/EducationLeadership/HowLeadershipInfluencesStudentLearning.htm

Littky, D. (2004). *The BIG picture: Education is everyone's business*. Alexandria, VA: ASCD.

Louis, K. S. (2007). *Changing the culture of schools: Professional community, organizational learning and trust*. Paper presented at Teacher Working Conditions that Matter: The Symposium. Elementary Teachers Federation of Ontario: Toronto, ON, Canada.

Louis, K., & Miles, M. (1990). *Improving the urban schools: What works and why*. New York: Falmer.

Martella, R., Nelson, R., & Marchand-Martella, N. (1999). *Research methods*. Toronto: Allyn & Bacon.

McLaughlin, M. (1990). The Rand change agent study revisited: Macro perspectives and micro realities. *Educational Researcher, 19*(9), 11–16.

McLaughlin, M., & Talbert, J. (2003). *Reforming districts: How districts support school reform*. University of Washington: Center for the Study of Teaching and Policy.

Mulford, W., Silins, H., & Leithwood, K. (2004). *Educational leadership for organizational learning and improved student outcomes*. Boston, MA: Kluwer.

Murphy, J., & Hallinger, P. (2001). Characteristics of instructionally effective school districts. *Journal of Educational Research, 81*(3), 175–181.

Popham, J. (2004). Swords with blunt edges. *Educational Leadership, 62*(4), 86–87.

Reeves, D. (2002). *The daily disciplines of leadership*. San Francisco, CA: Jossey-Bass.

Schein, E. (1992). *Organizational culture and leadership: A dynamic view*. San Francisco, CA: Jossey-Bass.

Schlechty, P. (2001). *Shaking up the school house*. San Francisco, CA: Jossey-Bass.

Schlechty, P. (2005). *Creating great schools: Six critical systems at the heart of educational innovation*. San Francisco, CA: Jossey-Bass.

Shaker, P., & Grimmett, P. (2004). Public schools as public good: A question of values. *Education Canada, 44*(3), 29–31.

Sheppard, B. (2003). If to do in schools were as easy as to know what were good to do. *Education Canada, 43*(4), 16–19.

Sheppard, B. (2008, September). *Schools as professional learning communities: Another simplistic fad or a worthwhile process?* Commonwealth Council for Educational Administration and Management (CCEAM), Durban, South Africa. Retrieved October 28, 2008 from http://www.emasa.co.za/ files/full/B.Sheppard2.pdf

Sheppard, B., & Brown, J. (1999, April). *Leadership approach, the new work of teachers and successful change*. Paper presented at the Annual Meeting of the American Educational Research Association, Montreal, Quebec, Canada. http://www.eric.ed.gov/. ED431229

Sheppard, B., & Brown, J. (2000a). Leadership and the transformation of secondary schools into learning organisations. In K. Leithwood (Ed.), *Understanding schools as intelligent systems* (pp. 293–314). Stamford, Connecticut: JAI Press.

Sheppard, B., & Brown, J.(2000b). So you think that team leadership is easy? Training and implementation concerns. *The NASSP Bulletin, 84*(614), 71–83.

Sheppard, B., & Brown, J. (2000c, April). *Pulling together or apart: Factors influencing a school's ability to learn*. Paper presented at the Annual Conference of the American Educational Research Association, New Orleans, US. http://www.eric.ed.gov/. ED443144.

Sheppard, B., & Brown, J. (2007, April). *The CEO as an emergent leader in a school district hierarchy: Challenges and opportunities*. Paper presented at American Educational Research Association, Chicago.

Spillane, J. (1996). School districts matter: Local educational authorities in state instructional policy. *Educational Policy, 10*(1), 63–87.

Starratt, R. (2004). *Ethical leadership*. San Francisco, CA: Jossey-Bass.

Stoll, L., & Fink, D. (1996). *Changing our schools*. Philadelphia: Open University Press.

Wang, M., & Walberg, H. (1991). Teaching and educational effectiveness: Research synthesis and consensus from the filed. In H. Waxman & H. Walberg (Eds.), *Effective teaching: Current research*. Berkeley, CA: McCurchan.

Chapter 2
Leadership and Organizational Learning

Abstract Leadership is seen as moving away from the traditional, hierarchical, rational planning, bureaucratic approach, toward a more collaborative approach with formal and informal leaders. Leadership and organizational learning are interrelated, with organizational learning being dependent on the capacity of the organization to facilitate collaboration among individual learners who take on distributed leadership responsibilities and learn from each other. The greatest challenge faced by school district is how to help schools become professional learning communities when the authoritarian hierarchy remained entrenched in the minds of formal leaders, community members, and government departments. Through a review of relevant empirical literature and reanalysis of five of their previous studies, the authors present a view of leadership that guided their actions and research in Discovery School District.

We view leadership as an organizational quality that is systemic and distributed throughout the organization (Ogawa & Bossert, 2000). Our understanding of leadership moves away from the traditional hierarchical, rational planning, bureaucratic approach toward a more collaborative approach in which there are two categories of leaders—formal leaders and informal leaders (constituents)[1] (Kouzes & Posner, 2003; Spillane, 2005b). In this approach to leadership, teachers are viewed as partners, rather than as followers, and leadership is defined through the interaction of leaders, constituents, and situation (Spillane, 2005a). Within this approach both formal leaders and constituents have an important, yet distinct, leadership role to play (York-Barr & Duke, 2004). Hall and Hord (2006) observe that

> In the learning organization context, all members of the staff share the leadership role, although the [formal] leader remains the point person. Ultimate responsibility must not be abandoned, and the positional leader (principal, superintendent, etc.) assumes and maintains this responsibility—but operationally in a less visible and more democratic way. (p. 31)

The formal leader must be transformational (Bass & Riggio, 2006), inclusive, value based, and focused on purposes that go beyond those that can be imagined

---

[1] We use the term *constituents* rather than *followers* consistent with Kouzes & Posner (2003) who believe that it better represents current understandings related to the relationship between formal leaders and others who within the traditional hierarchy have been viewed as followers.

individually and that transcend the surface noise of pettiness, contradiction, and self-interest (O'Toole, 1996). A successful school and district leader must focus on setting directions, developing people, and redesigning the organization (Leithwood, Louis, Anderson, & Wahlstrom, 2004). Toward that purpose, the formal leader must have a clear, uncompromising personal vision of where he/she wants the school or school district to go and how to get there. The vision must be focused on improving learning for each student. Everyone must understand that competence and commitment to student learning are nonnegotiable. In order to achieve this vision, the formal leader must have an in-depth understanding of the emerging theory related to leadership and organizational learning (Fullan, 2005a). He/she must establish and maintain credibility (Kouzes & Posner, 2003), must understand organizational and administrative theory (Hoy & Miskel, 2008) and change theory (Hall & Hord, 2006), must be an instructional leader (Blase & Blase, 1998; Leithwood et al.; Marks and Printy, 2003; Sheppard, 1996), and must be able to facilitate distributed leadership (Hallinger, 2005; Spillane, 2005a) and organizational learning (Fullan, 2005a). We have found that in addition to the overarching necessity of distributed leadership, the facilitation of organizational learning requires a focus on at least the following factors or conditions: (1) the development of a shared vision that is student focused; (2) a commitment to teaching and learning; (3) high expectations in a caring, inclusive culture; (4) a commitment to personal professional learning of all personnel; (5) the development of a collaborative culture; (6) an emphasis on action learning; and (7) the facilitation of systems thinking.

In this approach to leadership, organizational learning and leadership are interrelated. Leadership facilitates organizational learning and in turn is facilitated by it. Within this particular leadership–organizational learning framework, it is understood that organizations can learn only as individuals learn, but individual learning is not sufficient. "Organizational learning differs [from individual learning] in that it requires that knowledge have a shared, social construction common to all members of the school organization" (Louis, p. 4). Therefore, organizational learning is dependent on the capacity of the organization to facilitate collaboration among individual learners who assume distributed leadership responsibilities and learn from one another (Senge, 1990; Senge, Roberts, Ross, Smith, & Kleiner, 1994). Toward that purpose, a culture of trust must be established (Bryk & Schneider, 2003; Sebring & Bryk, 2000; Tschannen-Moran & Hoy, 2000) along with high expectations (Fullan, 2005a; Leithwood & Jantzi, 2005; Leithwood et al., 2004) that each individual contributes meaningfully toward the attainment of the organization's vision. Individuals must feel valued and supported by the formal leader who facilitates meaningful professional development, collaboration, self-appraisal, and action learning (Fullan, 2005a; Louis, 2007).

While the role of the formal leader as described above has received considerable attention in the literature, the role of constituents and the interrelationship between the two have not received the same attention (Heck & Hallinger, 1999; Spillane, Halverson, & Diamond, 2001; Spillane & Orlina, 2005). In the collaborative approach to leadership, the role of the second category of leaders (the constituents) and the interaction between constituents and the formal leader are recognized as being critical. Leadership success is contingent upon the perceptions that constituents have of the formal leader and his/her leadership behaviors (Blase & Blase, 1998; Burns, 1978; Foster, 1989; Gardner, 1990; Hallinger, 2005; Kouzes & Posner, 2003; Lord & Maher, 1990; Marks and Printy, 2003; Sheppard, 1996). If they do not share a common vision or if they are ignored by the formal leader, as is often the case in the traditional top-down leadership approach, constituents will neither share leadership nor follow voluntarily. In fact, it is not unusual for disenfranchised constituents to lead in directions that contradict those anticipated by the formal leader (Schlechty, 1997).

Unfortunately, the view of leadership and how organizations learn that we have described above is not a part of the most commonly accepted mindscapes of how organizations are organized and managed. More typical is a general acceptance of the traditional organizational model of hierarchical leadership as the best way; therefore, it cannot be assumed that formal leaders are willing to share leadership or that constituents will willingly engage in school leadership even if invited. In reality, the view of leadership as collaborative and distributed is a particularly challenging aspect of professional learning communities (Beachum & Dentith, 2004; Goldstein, 2004; Lieberman & Miller, 2005; Murphy, 2007; Sheppard, 2003b). "The dominant organizational metaphor of our time is still the hierarchy, organized by rank and authority" (Kouzes & Posner, 2003, p. 3), and the most popular acceptable leadership models focus on one person (usually charismatic) who engages in top-down management using one of three generic approaches to leadership: command, manipulate, and paternalize (O'Toole, 1996). It is not surprising, therefore, that most schools and school districts are bureaucratic hierarchies that are quite resistant to the empirically based leadership–organizational learning approach described above. "Teacher leaders ... will be only as successful as the bureaucracy allows them to be" (Pallicer & Anderson, 1995, p. 21) and "a shift in a typical school's culture toward a professional learning community will not occur through a year-long principal initiated work plan" (Louis, 2007, p. 5).

> Change is always accompanied by conflict, disequilibrium, and confusion. In the current era, shaped ... by dramatic changes in the world and dominated by a push toward accountability and standardization, change that calls for the development of professional communities and the emergence of teacher leadership may be even more difficult to achieve and maintain. (Lieberman & Miller, 2005, p. 161)

While making structural changes (organizational arrangements, procedures, rules, and policies) has been shown to be important to the facilitation of collaborative leadership and organizational learning, they are merely initial steps and will likely fail if there is no consideration of organizational and professional culture of schools and school systems (Mulford, Silins, & Leithwood, 2004; Schlechty, 1997; Sparks, 2005; York-Barr & Duke, 2004).

Murphy (2007) suggests that the bureaucratic, hierarchical structure presents a huge challenge to teacher leadership because it is deeply rooted in the professional culture. It benefits some people who are unwilling to give up the privileged position; it holds considerable legitimacy because it has worked for many students; and it is the only structure that most educators have known. This "vertical system of authority based on formal organizational roles" (Dunlap & Goldman, 1991, p. 5) is so firmly set in the professional culture that even when formal leaders do not visibly exercise such top-down power or influence, others expect it of them. Those working within that system will always resist and always fight to preserve the system (Dufour & Eaker, 1998, p. 49–50). Because hierarchy is so deeply imbedded as a professional norm of what is accepted as the role of formal leaders as compared to teachers, shifting to a more collaborative approach to leadership is much more than a simplistic issue of changing a structure.

There are other norms as well, related specifically to the professional work of teachers that militate against teacher leadership and organizational learning. These norms that rob teachers of "the energy that is essential to continuously improving teaching, learning, and relationships in schools" (Sparks, 2005, p. 10) include isolation, lack of clarity, teacher autonomy, followership and compliance, privacy and noninterference from inside or outside, dependence on routine, aversion to risk taking, and inverted beginner responsibilities (Glickman, Gordon, & Ross-Gordon, 2007; Murphy, 2007; Sparks, 2005).

In addition to the structural and cultural impediments that exist largely at the organizational level, there are challenges related to changes at the individual level as people feel threatened that they will not be able to function competently in a revised structure with new role expectations (Black & Gregersen, 2002; Lieberman & Miller, 2005). Considering the combined impediments—structural, cultural, and personal—it is not surprising that meaningful educational reform has been so difficult or that, after having assessed the organizational structures and culture of American schools, Elmore (2002) concluded that "the brutal irony of our present circumstance is that schools are hostile and inhospitable places for learning. They are hostile to the learning of adults and, because of this, they are necessarily hostile to the learning of students" (p. 5).

Confronting the Challenge

The challenge, then, is how to facilitate collaborative leadership and organizational learning in an environment where the authoritarian hierarchy and the professional norms related to the work of teachers remain deeply entrenched in the minds of formal leaders and followers as not only the best way but also the only way of organizing. Shifting away from the traditional hierarchical approach to leadership appears to be outside the existing mental models of most school professionals as there exists no established "cognitive frame through which to make sense (Weick, 1995) of teachers in [leadership] roles, despite the growing proliferation of teacher leadership [initiatives]" (Goldstein, 2004). The pervasive mental models of hierarchy and traditional formal leadership are powerful because they shape the way educators understand and interpret their world, and therefore, even those who appear to be willing to accept the potential of collaborative leadership often have difficulty making the shifts required as they grapple with unlearning that which they think they already know (Harris, 2005; Leavitt, 2003; Ogawa & Bossert, 2000; Sheppard, 2003b; Wheatley, 2000; York-Barr & Duke, 2004). "There are few precedents, few models, and no guidelines" (Lieberman, Saxl, & Miles, 2000, p. 348) for those who wish to make the shift. Recognizing this reality, Harris (2005) has concluded that

> "it" would be naïve to ignore the major structural, cultural, and micro-political barriers operating in schools . . . that make distributed forms of leadership difficult to implement. Clearly, schools as traditional hierarchies . . . are not going to be instantly responsive to a more fluid and distributed approach to leadership. (p. 260)

As a way forward, she suggests that formal leaders have a role in breaking down those barriers and states that "distributed leadership depends upon more formal leadership structures [and that, in fact] distributed leadership is unlikely to flourish unless those in formal leadership positions positively promote and support it" (p. 261). Similarly, Sparks (2005) contends that

> leaders matter in the creation and long-term maintenance of professional learning communities [as they can address the barriers of professional learning, and that, in fact], profound change in schools . . . begins with profound change in leaders that radiates out to others and into the system. (p. 10)

Sparks (2005) suggests that formal leaders can facilitate constituents' engagement in leadership by engaging them in dialogue and meaningful discussion in order to bring clarity in respect to their own values, intentions, and beliefs surrounding student learning. Sparks believes that as a result of their active participation in school leadership through dialogue and the development of shared visions for their own school, constituents will feel trusted and valued and therefore become confident that they can make a difference to student learning. Dialogue, as referenced above, is distinct from discussion, debate, and argument as the latter three often result in a perceived power imbalance and loss of trust that present themselves as barriers to genuine complex understanding (Bohm, 2007; Freire, 2004; Isaacs, 1999; Senge et al., 1994). Dialogue allows people to feel involved and welcomed; there is no hierarchy, equality of all participants is universally understood, and disagreement is encouraged. In such a context, individuals will feel that they are valued and respected for their views and, therefore, are more likely to feel that it is safe to express and explore differing views or ideas—even those ideas that are not fully developed.

Senge et al. (1994) share a similar view that when constituents perceive that the formal leader holds high expectations of their (the constituents) leadership role, when constituents feel valued and supported, and when they are given opportunities to engage in dialogue, they develop individually and collectively as leaders and thereby contribute to the organization's leadership capacity and to organizational learning. Unfortunately, the most commonly held interpretation of high expectations as being increased top-down accountability appears to be negatively associated with the development of constituents' leadership capacity (Argyris & Schön, 1978; Hendry, 1996; Senge et al., 1994). Hendry contends, for example, that when organizational cultures exert conformity and exercise control, they inhibit organizational learning because high expectations are often confused with top-down accountability that creates stress and negatively impacts personal learning. Argyris and Schön share that view as well. They argue that learning is inhibited when the environment is managed unilaterally, when people are discouraged from expressing negative feelings, and when rationality is valued at the expense of feelings. In professional learning communities, the importance of high expectations is based on an assumption that "in the right atmosphere, people will contribute and make commitments because they want to learn, to do good work for its own sake, and to be recognized as people" (Senge et al., p. 200). In order to create this "right atmosphere," it is essential that a formal leader consider the fundamental values and perspectives of followers and demonstrate respect for them by "always [practicing] the art of inclusion" (O'Toole, 1996, p. 37).

While we share the view that formal leaders are essential to the facilitation of collaborative leadership, evidence from several of our own investigations (Brown, Dibbon, & Sheppard, 2003; Brown & Sheppard, 1999; Sheppard & Brown, 1996, 1997, 1998, 1999, 2000a, 2000b, 2006, 2007a, 2007b; Sheppard, 2003a) has led us to conclude that not all formal leaders are aware of more distributed approaches to leadership or the empirical evidence related to organizational learning. Furthermore, we have come to realize that it is naïve to assume that those who are willing to accept the potential of such a leadership approach are able to practice it without effort or difficulty (Sheppard, 2003b, p. 17). In order to lead a shift to a new model, formal leaders must confront their own mental models at the same time as they facilitate the unlearning of those they lead—an inherently challenging process.

How Can Formal Leaders Facilitate Collaborative Leadership and Organizational Learning?

As a means of assessing how formal leaders can facilitate collaborative leadership and organizational learning practices in schools and school districts, we reanalyzed data and findings of five selected studies related to collaborative leadership and professional learning communities that Brown and I have conducted over the last decade or so (Sheppard, 1996; Brown & Sheppard, 1999; Sheppard & Brown, 2000a, 2000b; Sheppard, 2003a). While none of these previous studies were designed specifically to explore the question of how formal leaders can influence collaborative leadership practices, a reanalysis of each revealed considerable insight into this question.

Study One

Study one (Sheppard, 1996) was a survey investigation. Data were collected from a random sample of teachers ($n = 624$) in one Canadian province and analyzed using multiple regression. This study was focused on understanding the transformational effect of instructional leadership behaviors of school principals and selected school-level characteristics essential to the development of successful schools.

Findings from this study, consistent with other research (e.g., Kouzes & Posner, 2003; Lord & Maher, 1990), confirmed that leadership is contingent upon the perceptions of the constituents. Analysis revealed that the impact of the principal's instructional leadership behaviors on the level of teachers' commitment, professional involvement, and the extent to which they were innovative was modified by the extent to which teachers accepted the leadership behaviors as being appropriate. Burch and Spillane (2003) viewed this finding as evidence that "school leaders can create incentives for teachers to take collective responsibility for academic improvement" (p. 519), while Marks and Printy (2003) perceive it as evidence that "strong transformational leadership by the principal is essential in supporting the commitment of teachers [who] themselves can be barriers to the development of teacher leadership" (p. 393). We concur with both interpretations and view the findings as evidence of the importance of formal leaders in facilitating the engagement of teachers in school leadership and how such engagement can be achieved without any deliberate attempt by the formal leader (principal) to impose it. The distribution of leadership occurred as a result of an interaction between the leadership behaviors of the school principal and the existing "corridor of beliefs" of teachers that provided a filter through which they determined the appropriateness of the principal's leadership behaviors.

Study Two

In Study two (Brown & Sheppard, 1999), we collected and analyzed both qualitative and quantitative data from a representative sample of 13 schools across three school districts. School types included high schools, junior high schools, elementary schools, and all-grade schools. School size ranged from 185 to 870 students, with schools located in both rural and urban centers. We collected data through interviews and surveys. Analysis of the qualitative data included speculative analysis, classifying and categorizing, and concept formation (Woods, 1986), and we used the survey data to develop a series of descriptive tables to both confirm and complement our qualitative findings. Following our preliminary analysis of the data, we developed individual school reports that we presented to school teams for their feedback and interpretation. Finally, we used multiple regression analysis to develop a series of best-fitting models to explain variance in organizational learning categories accounted for by collaborative leadership.

We found that while collaborative leadership accounted for up to 45% of the variance of five indicators of organizational learning, it (collaborative leadership) was not a common phenomenon in the 13 schools in any of the three school districts. Most viewed the district's organizational learning focus to be just another project where data were collected for research purposes and not as data that could inform practice. Furthermore, even when formal leaders stated that they believed that organizational learning would facilitate meaningful change, many of them were unwilling or unable to make the shift in the leadership approach that was necessary. The ability of school administrators to make the shift appeared to be dependent on their understanding of collaborative leadership, the extent to which their constituents viewed collaborative leadership to be appropriate, and the administrators' ability to deal with other contextual variables and routine management issues. Many principals and teachers indicated that they were uncomfortable with shifting to a more collaborative leadership approach because they understood it to mean that the hierarchy would cease to exist. As a result, they feared that shifting away from their traditional top-down models would result in chaos as well as a perception of weakness. This fear resulted in their staying with the status quo even though some indicated that they felt there might be some merit in moving to a more collaborative approach to leadership. Also, we found that it was well-nigh impossible for teachers to engage in genuine collaborative leadership activities without the endorsement of the school principal. In one school, for example, a teacher who was a member of the school leadership team, when asked to draw an image of how she perceived leadership in her school, drew an inverted triangle (see Fig. 2.1). She explained that the width of the triangle base represented power and placed the principal at that widest point. She placed herself as a tiny dot outside of the triangle tip at the bottom of the inverted triangle and explained emotionally that she felt that neither she nor other members of the team had any real influence in spite of their best efforts. Obviously, in this particular school, the vertical system of authority continued to overpower even those teachers who were committed to being school leaders. This latter finding was disruptive to our thinking at the time of our first analysis because we had been operating with the assumption that the development of collaborative leadership in a school could overcome obstacles imposed by the most dominant of school principals. Currently, we are convinced that while it might fall within the realm of being possible, it is certainly unlikely that collaborative leadership will flourish in environments where it is resisted by the principal.

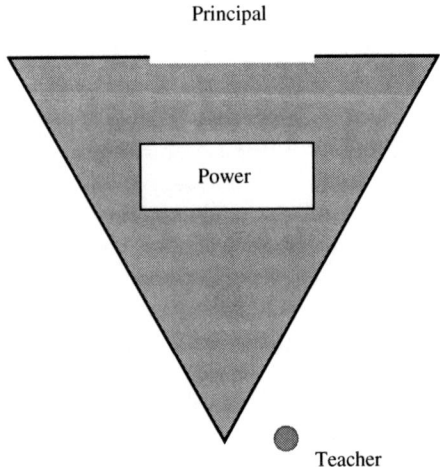

Fig. 2.1 A teacher's depiction of leadership

Study Three

Both Study three (Sheppard & Brown, 2000a) and Study four (Sheppard & Brown, 2000b) are school case studies. Study three was a two-year case study of an alternate school for young offenders where we were invited by the school's administrators to engage in a research and development partnership initiative in order to facilitate organizational learning. Employing a participatory action research model (Whyte, Greenwood, & Lazes, 1991), our data sources included 34 interviews, document analysis, field notes from participant observations of 17 leadership team meetings, journal notes from regular consultations with two key informants, and surveys completed by 94 of the approximate 100 employees. For analysis, we used a variety of analytical methods including a constant comparative method, theoretical memos, clustering of conceptual groupings and corresponding matrices (Glaser & Strauss, 1967; Miles & Huberman, 1994; Strauss & Corbin, 1994). Similar to our approach in Study two, following our preliminary analysis of the available data, we prepared a report that we shared with the school action research team, thereby allowing our analysis and interpretations to be corrected and verified.

At the first meeting of the leadership team, we asked members to engage in small group brainstorming sessions to identify factors that they considered to be barriers to organizational improvement. The most pronounced identified inhibitor of organizational learning and distributed leadership was the absence of trust among constituents and between the formal leaders and constituents. Of seven distinct groups of constituents, each appeared to be suspicious of the other. Teachers thought that the social workers had more influence than they did. Support staff felt that teachers held an elitist attitude toward others in the organization and that they (teachers) thought that others had nothing worthwhile to contribute to the students' education. The teachers, social workers, support staff, and nurses thought that the counselors were concerned only for their own welfare. All nonmanagement groups felt that the administrators were plotting against them, and only 16% of the employees thought that everyone's ideas were given equal weight. It was obvious that constituents did not feel valued, were not engaged in dialogue, and did not feel supported. Overall, the collaborative engagement of constituents in leadership was practically nonexistent, and several support staff union members were emphatic that they did not trust the other individuals on the leadership team and would not be manipulated into any pretense of sharing leadership in the organization. It was obvious that the social trust essential for meaningful school improvement (Bryk & Schneider, 2003; Sebring & Bryk, 2000) was nonexistent. Representatives of neither group were confident that other group members, especially the school's administrators, were open, honest, reliable, competent, or benevolent—essential characteristics of trust in an organization (Tschannen-Moran & Hoy, 2000)—and therefore were unwilling to allow themselves to be vulnerable to other group members.

Over the course of the two-year period of the partnership initiative, the leadership team learned about organizational learning and focused on increasing the level of collaborative leadership. The administrators made commitments to meaningful engagement with constituents, to cultivating trust by being more consistent in management practices, to sharing power with the leadership team, and to communicating more openly and honestly with all constituents (Whitener, Brodt, Korsgaard, & Werner, 1998). Toward the end of that first two-year period, it appeared that the team had been somewhat effective in the introduction of dialogue—at least at the leadership team level—and as a result, levels of trust and the extent to which individuals felt valued had improved throughout the organization. For example, one of the leadership team members observed:

> It has made a real difference to those of us on the learning organization team. I think that it has made a real difference.... We have involved counselors, kitchen staff, secretarial staff, social worker staff, and counselors, all the way through this facility.... It has opened up a whole new world for me.... I like the direction that it's going. (Sheppard & Brown, 2000a, p. 5)

The assistant director was quite optimistic about the improved level of trust and collaboration that occurred as a result of the deliberate focus on meaningfully including constituents as leaders in the facilitation of organizational learning:

> One of the key things that has happened over the past year and a half that is directly associated with our work on learning organizations is an opening up of the boundaries between the professions within the organization. Three or four years ago they were closed camps. There was little sharing between the groups. There was a great deal of stress associated with interaction between the groups. Since we've started exploring ourselves and looking at who we are and working together as a team, there is much more sharing now than in the past. That is directly related to our work in learning organizations. That comes from looking at ourselves and talking about it with each other. (Sheppard & Brown, 2000a, p. 5)

While this organization was a traditional hierarchy that was deeply troubled, the formation of a leadership team composed of formal leaders and constituents proved invaluable to the building of trust and the facilitation of organizational learning. While the findings of this study reveal the difficulty of changing to a more collaborative approach to leadership, particularly when trust levels are low, it also reveals the important role of formal leaders in initiating positive change in the leadership approach. In fact, without the willingness of the formal leader (the assistant administrator) to engage in an initiative to facilitate collaborative leadership and organizational learning, it is highly likely that the low trust levels and accompanying dysfunctional behaviors would have continued. Even after realizing considerable success, the chief administrator continued to struggle to overcome his deeply ensconced mental model of hierarchical leadership that prevented him from meaningfully sharing leadership. Similarly, the extent to which constituents who were not members of the leadership team expressed support or skepticism for a more collaborative leadership approach varied greatly throughout the organization.

Study Four

In Study four (Sheppard & Brown, 2000b), we studied two high schools that had national reputations as innovative schools. Our data collection included interviews, document analysis, and the administration of a leadership survey. We interviewed a total of 32 teachers and two administrators and reviewed staff meeting minutes, school improvement committee minutes, school improvement plans, newspaper clippings, daily school announcements, and school academic achievement reports. We conducted our data analysis through the development of complex causal networks (Miles & Huberman, 1994) through which we traced approximately 10 years of school improvement efforts in each of these schools.

We concluded that both schools had sustained successful organizational development over the course of the 10-year period that we studied. At the beginning of the decade, both schools had been traditional bureaucracies that had struggled with low student achievement; however, as a consequence of the active intervention of principals (formal leaders), a shift toward a more collaborative approach to leadership occurred during our study period. While competent leadership provided by the principal was important in both schools, sustainability of each school's success over the course of the decade was dependent on a robust norm of collaborative leadership. In both schools, the person filling the role of principal changed several times during that period. Given the empirical evidence that it is not uncommon for schools to experience a dip in the level of trust between constituents and the formal leader during succession (Macmillan, Meyer & Northfield, 2007), we expected to observe a dip in collaborative leadership with each principal's succession. However, in these schools there remained a continuity of focus that allowed for sustained learning. It appears that the sustainability of their success was highly dependent on the appointment of successive principals who were supportive of the established culture of collaborative leadership and the continued existence of structures and processes that supported it. "These processes allowed [each] leader to build systemically on what his/her successor had accomplished and each leader demonstrated a willingness to take on this task, rather than embarking on some entirely new set of priorities as is most often the case" (Sheppard & Brown, 2000b, p. 313).

Study Five

Study five (Sheppard, 2003a) was a case study of 15 schools that had been involved in a national project directed at the integration of emerging technologies into teaching and learning. Because the intent of the national project was to bring about significant changes to the teaching and learning process, these project schools provided an excellent venue for the study of the factors that facilitate or inhibit change at the classroom level. One researcher spent three days in each of the schools gathering data through field notes of observations and through semi-structured interviews with the principal, the technology teacher, the teacher-librarian, other selected teachers, and students. We conducted 92 interviews: 15 principals, 46 teachers, 27 groups of students, and 4 members of the project headquarters staff. For our data analysis we followed an approach similar to that employed in study three described above (Glaser & Strauss, 1967; Miles & Huberman, 1994; Strauss & Corbin, 1994).

We found that the six schools that had been identified as innovative displayed more collaborative leadership approaches than the other nine less-innovative schools. While the formal leader in the innovative schools was important to the successful implementation of emerging technologies in teaching and learning, the leadership influence was greater when it was indirect. In schools that were most successful in altering classroom practices through the use of emerging technologies, the principals were focused on distributing leadership that fostered cultures conducive to organizational learning. In those innovative schools, the principals were not necessarily the champions of the specific change initiative; however, they were champions of capacity building and collaborative leadership. They found ways for teachers to learn on the job and encouraged all to be instructional leaders. As a result, leadership was distributed among many teachers (constituents) who assumed leadership responsibility for the change initiative. These teachers felt empowered to act without seeking permission of the formal leaders and were not threatened by the risk of failure.

In contrast to the innovative schools, change did not occur in static schools in spite of community and district pressures. Implementation of emerging technologies in classrooms was somewhat restricted in the moderately innovative schools as well. In both static and moderately innovative schools, leadership remained primarily the responsibility and prerogative of formal leaders who employed the traditional hierarchical approach to leadership. While individual teachers with the necessary expertise existed in most of the 15 schools, without the encouragement or support of their school principal, these teachers assumed little responsibility for leadership of the implementation outside of their own classrooms, and when they departed the school, implementation stalled. While it is difficult to determine the extent to which teachers in the innovative schools were more predisposed to engage as leaders than those in other schools or whether their engagement in leadership resulted from some facilitating action of the formal leader, what is certain is that, unlike the static schools, leadership in the innovative schools was distributed and that distribution of leadership was supported by the principals.

Implications for the Implementation and Practice of Collaborative Leadership

Spillane (2005b) has stated that the theoretical study of distributed leadership must include consideration of formal and informal leaders and the practices of those leaders. We concur with him on that account, and furthermore, we contend that the same applies to the implementation and practice of collaborative leadership. From a pragmatic perspective, shifting to a collaborative approach to leadership and engaging constituents as leaders (distributing leadership) will not occur automatically as a result of theorizing or decree, or by just providing the opportunity. Formal leaders who are committed to a collaborative leadership approach must consider leadership as "a product of the interactions of school leaders, [constituents and formal leaders], and their situation" (Spillane, 2005b, p. 385).

Most school districts and schools continue to operate as traditional hierarchical bureaucracies; therefore, the common expectation is that someone at the top of the organization will set the direction. Simply stating that an organization is now going to be collaborative, that leadership will be distributed, and that all constituents will now be leaders will most likely result in failure. Without shared images of these new practices, formal leaders and constituents are likely to be overwhelmed by "the inertia of deeply entrenched mental models" (Senge, 1990, p. 77). A formal leader who is committed to a collaborative leadership approach must focus on establishing a culture of collaboration and trust throughout a school or school district and must work with constituents to both develop shared images of the organization they wish to create and eliminate the barriers imposed by the structures and processes of the traditional hierarchy. While it can be anticipated that a formal leader who is committed to a collaborative approach will encounter resistance to this shift from some other formal leaders and those constituents who remain wedded to the traditional hierarchy, there is growing empirical evidence, including the five studies reviewed above, that suggests that a formal leader can facilitate the engagement of constituents as leaders. However, there appears to be no single pattern of how this might occur.

In study one above, the formal leader engaged in leadership behaviors that constituents perceived to be meaningful to their work, and as a result they became more professionally involved and were more committed to improved teaching practices. The importance of constituents' perceptions of the appropriateness of the formal leader's behaviors was apparent in studies two and three as well. In study two, the majority of the formal leaders and constituents remained skeptical of any movement away from the traditional hierarchical practices. As a result, an awareness of collaborative leadership approaches did not easily translate into a change in practices. While constituents who were committed to a collaborative leadership approach may have been able to facilitate a shift in that direction, it appeared that the processes and structures of hierarchy were so deeply imbedded into the mindscapes of the majority that any challenge to its legitimacy would likely have been thwarted by formal leaders who resisted sharing leadership. Similarly, study three revealed how the deeply imbedded dependence of both constituents and formal leaders on the traditional administrative hierarchical organizational structures limited their ability to seek solutions outside of that framework even when constituent groups and administrators recognized that their school was in difficulty. While trust was not common currency either among the various constituent groups or between the constituents and formal leaders, both the lack of trust and the blame for the school's problems were attributed almost entirely to the formal leaders. Yet, paradoxically, in spite of their lack of confidence in the school's administrators and mistrust in their motives, constituents remained dependent on the normal chain of command of the traditional hierarchical structures for solutions. The subsequent shift to organizational learning at this particular school, however, revealed the importance of knowledge acquisition from external sources (Dibella, Nevis, & Gould, 1996) and highlighted both the extent of the influence of a formal leader in the facilitation of collaborative leadership (Schein, 2004) and the potential positive impact of a leadership team of formal leaders and constituents on increased leadership capacity. As a result of the distribution of leadership within the leadership team, it became somewhat effective in overcoming some of the defensive routines that had perpetuated the hiding of the "undiscussables" that were imbedded in the organization (Argyris & Schön, 1991; Hendry, 1996; Senge, 1990).

Studies four and five revealed the potential of the formal leader to either inhibit or facilitate collaborative leadership. In study four, we observed that two principals who were committed to a collaborative leadership approach worked with constituents to design structures and processes that facilitated the distribution of leadership among constituents. As a result, collaborative leadership was sustained over a period of 10 years and even withstood several successive principals. Study five allowed us to contrast the impact of varying degrees of collaborative leadership on the implementation of classroom innovation. This study revealed clearly that the formal leader and the extent to which he/she was committed to collaborative leadership had a major impact on the engagement of other teachers (constituents) in leadership activities. Schools where the formal leader was supportive of collaborative leadership benefited from it and successfully implemented emerging technologies as part of the teaching and learning process. On the other hand, schools where leadership was viewed as the principal's role were generally unsuccessful in their implementation efforts.

Another finding from this work, while not new, is that leadership is not zero-summed (e.g., Dunlap & Goldman, 1991; Roberts, 1986). This finding represents a further challenge to those that fear that chaos will result if formal leaders "give up" power in order to share it with constituents. In study two and study four, an increase in constituents' involvement in leadership did not lead to a decrease in the formal leader's influence; rather the opposite occurred. As leadership became more distributed over a larger group of constituents and as their level of influence increased, the extent to which the formal leader was perceived to provide leadership grew accordingly.

It is evident that the traditional hierarchical structures remain pervasive in schools. Equally evident is that the structures and the mental models held by those who work within them continue to present major barriers to the acceptance of collaborative leadership approaches and organizational learning. Fortunately, there is considerable evidence as well that formal leaders who are committed to collaborative approaches to leadership can influence constituents' level of engagement in leadership in spite of these barriers. The theoretical foundations of collaborative leadership and organizational learning offer real promise for the improvement of our schools; however, attention must be given to the complexities related to the implementation of such a "disruptive innovation" (Schlechty, 2005). Simplistically adopting the lexicon of collaborative leadership and professional learning community and approaching implementation as an event are likely to result in "not finding any significant differences ... [and concluding] that the new approach does not work" (Hall & Hord, 2006, p. 5) when, in fact, neither collaborative learning nor organizational learning was implemented in the first place.

It is our view that if collaborative leadership and organizational learning are to become more than a random and rare phenomenon, they need to be led by senior leaders at the school district level. They are best positioned to implement deliberate strategies of pressure, interventions, and support that are required to bring about the required changes in roles, structures, and organizational norms within and across large numbers of schools (Elmore, 2002; Fullan, 2005b; Hightower, Knapp, Marsh, & McLaughlin, 2002; Peterson & Cosner, 2005; Phelps & Addonizio, 2006). It is this view of leadership that guided our actions and research within Discovery School District.

References

Argyris, C., & Schön, D. (1978). *Organizational learning: A theory of action perspective.* Don Mills, Ont.: Addison-Wesley.
Argyris, C., & Schön, D. (1991). Participatory action research and action science compared: A commentary. In Whyte, W. F. (Ed.), *Participatory action research* (pp. 85–96). Newbury Park: Sage.
Bass, B., & Riggio, R. (2006). *Transformational leadership.* Mahwah, NJ: Lawrence Erlbaum.
Beachum, F., & Dentith, A. (2004). Teacher leaders creating cultures of school renewal and transformation. *The Educational Forum, 68*(3), 276–286.
Black, S., & Gregersen, H. (2002). *Leading strategic change: Breaking through the brain barriers.* New York: Prentice Hall.
Blase, J., & Blase, J. (1998). *Handbook of instructional leadership: How really good principals promote teaching and learning.* Thousand Oaks, CA: Corwin.
Bohm, M. (2007). *On dialogue.* New York, NY: Routledge.
Brown, J., Dibbon, D., & Sheppard, B. (2003, May). *The school trustee in a learning environment.* Halifax, NS, Canada: Annual Conference of CSSE.
Brown, J., & Sheppard, B. (1999, April). *Leadership, organizational learning, and classroom change.* Paper presented at the Annual Conference of the American Educational Research Association, Montreal, Quebec, Canada. ED431230. Retrieved on April 22, 2007 from http://www.eric.ed.gov/
Bryk, A. S., & Schneider, B. (2003). Trust in schools: A core resource for school reform. *Educational Leadership, 60*(6), 40–44.
Burch, P., & Spillane, J. (2003). Elementary school leadership strategies and subject matter: Reforming mathematics and literacy instruction. *The Elementary School Journal, 103*(5), 519–535.
Burns, J. M. (1978). *Leadership.* New York: Harper & Row.
Dibella, A. J., Nevis, E. C., & Gould, J. M. (1996). Understanding organizational learning capacity. *Journal of Management Studies, 33*(3), 361–379.
Dufour, R., & Eaker, R. (1998). *Professional learning communities at work: Best practices for enhancing student achievement.* Alexandria, CA: Association for Supervision and Curriculum Development.
Dunlap, D., & Goldman, P. (1991, February). Rethinking power in schools. *Educational Administration Quarterly, 27*(1), 5–29.
Elmore, R. (2002) *Bridging the gap between standards and achievement: The imperative for professional development in education.* Washington, DC: Albert Shanker Institute.
Foster, (1989). Toward a critical practice of leadership. In J. Smyth (Ed.), *Critical perspectives in educational leadership* (pp. 39–62). London: The Falmer Press.
Freire, P. (2004). Pedagogy of the oppressed. In D. J. Flinders & S. J. Thornton (Eds.), *The curriculum studies reader* (pp. 125–133). New York: Routledge Falmer.

Fullan, M. (2005a). *Leadership and sustainability*. Thousand Oaks, CA: Corwin.
Fullan, M. (2005b). Turnaround leadership. *The Educational Forum, 69*(2), 174–181.
Gardner, J. (1990). *On leadership*. New York, NY: Free Press.
Glaser, B., & Strauss, A. (1967). *The discovery of grounded theory: Strategies for qualitative research*. Chicago: Aldine.
Glickman, C., Gordon, S., & Ross-Gordon, J. (2007). *SuperVision of instructional leadership: A developmental approach*. Needham Heights, MA: Allyn & Bacon.
Goldstein, J. (2004). Making sense of distributed leadership: The case of peer assistance and review. *Educational Evaluation and Policy Analysis, 26*(2), 173–197.
Hall, G., & Hord S. (2006). *Implementing change: Patterns, principles, and potholes*. Toronto: Pearson Education.
Hallinger, P. (2005). *Instructional leadership: How has the model evolved?* Paper presented at the Annual Conference of the American Educational Research Association, Montreal, Quebec, Canada.
Harris, A. (2005). OP-ED. *Journal of Curriculum Studies, 37*(3), 255–265.
Heck, R. H., & Hallinger, P. (1999). Next generation methods for the study of leadership and school improvement. In J. Murphy & K. Louis (Eds.), *Handbook of educational administration* (pp. 141–162). New York: Longman.
Hendry, C. (1996). Understanding and creating whole organizational change through learning theory. *Human Relations, 49*(5), 621–641.
Hightower, A., Knapp, M., Marsh, J., & McLaughlin, M. (2002). The district role in instructional renewal: Setting the stage for dialogue. In A. Hightower, M. Knapp, J, Marsh, & M. McLaughlin (Eds.), *School districts and instructional renewal*. New York: Teachers College.
Hoy, W., & Miskel, C. (2008) *Educational administration: Theory, research and practice*. New York: McGraw Hill.
Isaacs, W. (1999). *Dialogue and the art of thinking together*. New York: Doubleday.
Kouzes, J., & Posner, B. (2003). *Credibility*. San Francisco, CA: Jossey-Bass.
Leavitt, H. (2003). Why hierarchies thrive. *Harvard Business Review*, March, 96–102.
Leithwood, K., & Jantzi, D. (2005). *A review of transformational school leadership research 1996–2005*. Paper presented at the annual meeting of the American Educational Research Association, Montreal, Canada.
Leithwood, K., Louis, K., Anderson, S., & Wahlstrom, K. (2004). *How leadership influences student learning*. Retrieved Nov. 28, 2005 from http://www.wallacefoundation.org/WF/KnowledgeCenter/KnowledgeTopics/EducationLeadership/ HowLeadershipInfluencesStudentLearning.htm
Lieberman, A., & Miller, L. (2005) Teachers as leaders. *The Educational Forum 69*(2), 151–162.
Lieberman, A., Saxl, E., & Miles, M. (2000). Teacher leadership: Ideology and practice. In *The Jossey-Bass reader on educational leadership* (pp. 348–365). San Francisco, CA: Jossey-Bass.
Lord, R., & Maher, K. (1990). Perceptions of leadership and their implications in organizations. In J. Carroll (Ed.), *Applied social psychology and organizational settings* (pp. 129–154). Hillsdale, NJ: Lawrence Erlbaum.
Louis, K. S. (2007). *Changing the culture of schools: Professional community, organizational learning and trust*. Paper presented at Teacher Working Conditions that Matter: The Symposium. Toronto, ON, Canada.
Macmillan, R., Meyer, M., & Northfield, S. (2007). *Trust, mistrust and distrust: A negotiation of meaning during principal succession*. Paper presented at the annual meeting of the Canadian Association for the Study of Educational Administration. Saskatoon, SK, Canada.
Marks, H., & Printy, S. (2003). Principal leadership and school performance: An integration of transformation and instructional leadership. *Educational Administration Quarterly, 39*(3), 370–397.
Miles, M., & Huberman, A. (1994). *Qualitative data analysis: A sourcebook of new methods*. Beverly Hills, CA: Sage.

References

Mulford, W., Silins, H., & Leithwood, K. (2004). *Educational leadership for organizational learning and improved student outcomes.* Boston, MA: Kluwer.

Murphy, J. (2007, June). *Teacher leadership: Barriers and supports.* Paper presented at Teacher Working Conditions that Matter: The Symposium. Toronto, ON, Canada.

Ogawa, R., & Bossert, S. (2000). Leadership as an organizational quality. In *The Jossey-Bass reader on educational leadership* (pp. 38–58). San Francisco, CA: Jossey-Bass.

O'Toole, J. (1996). *Leading change.* Toronto: Jossey-Bass.

Pellicer, L., & Anderson, L. (1995). *A handbook for teacher leaders.* Thousand Oaks, CA: Corwin.

Peterson, K., & Cosner, S. (2005). Teaching your principal. *Journal of Staff Development, 26*(2), 28–32.

Phelps, J., & Addonizio, M. (2006). How much do school districts matter? A production function approach to school accountability. *Educational Considerations, 33*(2), 51–61.

Roberts, N. C. (1986). Organizational power styles: Collective and competitive power under varying organizational conditions. *The Journal of Applied Behavioral Science, 22*(4), 443–458.

Schein, E. (2004). *Organizational culture and leadership.* San Fransico, CA: Jossey-Bass.

Schlechty, P. (1997). *Inventing better schools: An action plan for education reform.* San Francisco, CA: Jossey-Bass.

Schlechty, P. (2005). *Creating great schools: Six critical systems at the heart of educational innovation.* San Francisco, CA: Jossey-Bass.

Sebring, P. B., & Bryk, A. S. (2000). School leadership and the bottom line in Chicago. *Phi Delta Kappan, 81*(6), 440–443.

Senge, P. (1990). *The fifth discipline.* New York: Doubleday.

Senge, P., Roberts, C, Ross, R, Smith, B., & Kleiner, A. (1994). *The fifth discipline fieldbook.* Toronto: Doubleday.

Sheppard, B. (1996). Exploring the transformational nature of instructional leadership. *Alberta Journal of Educational Research, 42*(4), 325–344.

Sheppard, B. (2003a). Leadership that fosters organizational learning proves critical to the successful integration of information and communication technology in teaching and learning. *International Electronic Journal for Leadership in Learning, 7*(14). Retrieved September 20, 2006 from http://www.ucalgary.ca/~iejll

Sheppard, B. (2003b). If to do in schools were as easy as to know what were good to do. *Education Canada, 43*(4), 16–19.

Sheppard, B., & Brown, J. (1996). Taylor High: An emerging learning organization. *The Canadian Administrator, 36*(3), 1–7.

Sheppard, B., & Brown, J. (1997, June). *Organizational learning: Connecting classroom practices and team leadership.* Paper presented at the Annual Conference of CSSE, St. John's, NF, Canada.

Sheppard, B., & Brown, J. (1998). Meeting the challenge of information technology through educational partnerships: A case study. *International Electronic Journal for Leadership in Learning, 2*(11).

Sheppard, B., & Brown, J. (1999, April). *Leadership approach, the new work of teachers and successful change.* Paper presented at the Annual Meeting of the American Educational Research Association, Montreal, Quebec, Canada.

Sheppard, B., & Brown, J. (2000a). Leadership and the transformation of secondary schools into learning organisations. In K. Leithwood (Ed), *Understanding schools as intelligent systems* (pp. 293–314). Stamford, Connecticut: JAI Press.

Sheppard, B., & Brown, J. (2000b, April). *Pulling together or apart: Factors influencing a school's ability to learn.* Paper presented at the Annual Conference of the American Educational Research Association, New Orleans, LA. (ERIC Document Reproduction Service No. ED443144). Retrieved on April 12, 2007 from http://www.eric.ed.gov/.

Sheppard, B., & Brown, J. (2006, October). *A CEO's five year journey: Translating theory into practice.* Paper presented at Commonwealth Council for Educational Administration and Management, Nicosia, Cyprus.

Sheppard, B., & Brown, J. (2007a, April). *The CEO as an emergent leader in a school district hierarchy: Challenges and opportunities*. Paper presented at American Educational Research Association, Chicago.

Sheppard, B., & Brown, J. (2007b, May). *Developing and implementing a shared vision of teaching and learning at the district level*. Paper presented at the Annual Conference of CSSE, Saskatoon, SK, Canada.

Sparks, D. (2005). The final 2%. *Journal of Staff Development, 26*(2), 8–15.

Spillane, J. (2005a). Distributed leadership. *The Educational Forum, 69*(2), 143–150.

Spillane, J. (2005b). Primary school leadership practice: How the subject matters. *School Leadership and Management, 25*(4), 383.

Spillane, J., Halverson, R., & Diamond, J. (2001). Investigating school leadership practice: A distributed perspective. *Educational Researcher, 30*(3), 23–28.

Spillane, J., & Orlina, E. (2005). *Investigating leadership practice: Exploring the entailments of taking a distributed perspective*. Paper presented at American Educational Research Association, Montreal, Canada.

Strauss, A., & Corbin, J. (1994). Grounded theory methodology: An overview. In N. Denzin & Y. Lincoln (Eds.), *Handbook of qualitative research* (pp. 273–285). Thousand Oaks, CA: Sage.

Tschannen-Moran, M., & Hoy, W. K. (2000). A multidisciplinary analysis of the nature, meaning, and measurement of trust. *Review of Educational Research, 70*(4), 547–593.

Weick, K. E. (1995). *Sensemaking in organizations*. Thousand Oaks, CA: Sage Publications.

Wheatley, M. (2000). Good-bye, command and control. In *The Jossey-Bass reader on educational leadership* (pp.339–347). San Francisco, CA: Jossey-Bass.

Whitener, E. M., Brodt, S. E., Korsgaard, M. A., & Werner, J. M. (1998). Managers as initiators of trust: An exchange relationship framework for understanding managerial trustworthy behavior. *Academy of Management Review, 23*, 513–530.

Whyte, W. F., Greenwood, D. J., & Lazes, P. (1991). Participatory action research: Through practice to science in social research. In Whyte, W. F. (Ed.), *Participatory action research* (pp. 19–55). Newbury Park, CA: Sage.

Woods, P. (1986). *Inside schools: Ethnography in educational research*. London: Routledge & Kagan Paul.

York-Barr, J. & Duke, K. (2004). What do we know about teacher leadership? Findings from two decades of scholarship. *Review of Educational Research, 74*(3), 255–316.

Chapter 3
Meeting the Challenges of Hierarchy Through District Leadership

Abstract School districts tend to operate as traditional hierarchical bureaucracies that are highly resistant to collaborative leadership and processes necessary for organizational learning. The literature review and this district case study reveal that, paradoxically, it is only by accepting this reality that school districts can move toward more collaborative leadership. It is this inherent paradox of working within the norms of hierarchy while altering the organizational structures to support collaborative leadership and organizational learning that poses great difficulty for formal leaders. It is risky, complex work. This case study also reveals the risk in doing collaborative research as a critical friend and the effects in a school district when an academic researcher returns to practice.

As noted in the previous chapter, over the last few years, the promise of organizational learning and more collaborative models of leadership for schools and school districts have been highly touted in the professional literature as a means of improving student learning. In spite of such literature and the growing empirical evidence of the positive effects of collaborative leadership and the coexisting organizational learning, neither has found its way into mainstream practice of chief executive officers (CEOs) in corporations, governments, schools, or school districts (Leavitt, 2003). These organizations, for the most part, continue to operate as traditional hierarchical bureaucracies that are highly resistant to collaborative leadership and processes that are essential to organizational learning. Miller's (1984) description of the CEO as the *Lone Ranger* poignantly illustrates the most popularly accepted leadership model that is focused on one person who is expected to have superhuman leadership capacities to deal successfully with all organizational challenges. Miller argues that CEOs and managers of organizations have learned from the model presented by this cultural hero of several decades ago. He observes that emulating this cultural hero, managers have assumed responsibility to personally diagnose organizational problems and to resolve them as soon as possible. Moreover, it appears that formal leaders and constituents in many organizations have accepted the assumption that constituents are incapable of resolving routine problems and that the measure of a formal leader's success is largely dependent upon his/her superior abilities to resolve problems for them. Miller suggests that such an approach to management is dependent upon the maintenance of a perception among constituents that the CEO or manager has some superior mystical powers that enable him/her to resolve these routine organizational problems. The Lone Ranger accomplished his mystique through the use of a mask. CEOs and managers strive to replicate this effect by remaining somewhat aloof from their constituents. Existence of such mindscapes in our organizations and governments that perpetuate the constant search for the charismatic hero presents a huge challenge to the implementation of collaborative leadership approaches.

Overcoming Resistance to Collaborative Leadership Through District Leadership

Within the context of the deeply entrenched cultural norms and structures that perpetuate the acceptance of the traditional hierarchical organizational structures and top-down management approaches, O'Toole (1996) asks, "How can ... a CEO ... overcome resistance to change [to a differing model of leadership] when the CEO's power is constrained by diverse and conflicting interests of investors, board members, union chiefs, environmentalists, government regulators, and careerist fellow managers, all intent on marching to the beat of their own drummers?" (p. 7). As far as schools are concerned, our response to O'Toole's question is that collaborative leadership and organizational learning are unlikely to occur at the school level in any pervasive fashion without school district intervention and support. While there are some examples of successful schools that are professional learning communities, these are isolated cases that appear to have had minimal impact on the overall public education. If collaborative leadership and organizational learning are to become the norm for schools, rather than something that occurs randomly in isolated cases as appears to be the current circumstance, the school district has the most potential for fostering that change. Attempting to develop the needed capacity one school at a time is akin to throwing pebbles in the Atlantic Ocean with the hope of building a causeway to connect the east coast of Canada to the UK. This is not to suggest, however, that researchers and policymakers should ignore the role of the school in efforts to improve public education, or to suggest that districts are better at organizational learning or overcoming the norms of hierarchy than schools. In fact, it may be that currently the contrary is true (Rusch, 2005). Our argument is that if the school district does not engage in organizational learning, it will most likely present itself as a major barrier to it in all of its schools. Besides, more leverage is possible if focus is placed on understanding how whole school districts, with all of their schools, can engage in organizational learning so they can provide leadership to individual schools that differ in their individual capacity to learn.

Contrary to our above-noted view, some writers have been quite pessimistic about the potential of school districts to foster school improvement (Berends, Bodilly, & Kirby, 2002; Bogatch & Brooks, 1994; Chubb & Moe, 1990; Doyle & Finn, 1984; Tewel, 1995). Anderson (2003) draws attention to the fact that school districts have "disappeared from the scene in New Zealand and school ties to local education authorities [have become] optional in England [thereby reminding us] that the school district is a political and organizational invention, not a natural and inevitable phenomenon, and that it is therefore quite reasonable to question and critique the role that districts can play in promoting and sustaining quality education" (p. 3). Besides, Rusch (2005) cites multiple studies that have found that school boards are centralized institutionalized bureaucracies that have been identified "as the major inhibitor of the dialogue or problem solving required for system-level restructuring or cross-system organizational learning" (p. 87).

In spite of such pessimism regarding the potential of school districts to facilitate school reform, even those who have advocated for changing one school at a time because of the perceived intransigence of school boards have recognized the need for some facilitating agency beyond the school (Elliott, 2001; Murphy, 2007; Rusch, 2005; Smylie, Conley, & Marks, 2002). Rusch (2005) observes that as a result of this recognition, multiple national coalitions and networks have been established in various jurisdictions. While there is evidence that these newly formed networks have had positive effects, Rusch (2005) found that school boards that operated as centralized institutionalized bureaucracies continued to inhibit organizational learning even in those schools that were involved in external networks. As a result, she questions the wisdom of ignoring school districts, suggesting that the long-term benefit of networks is questionable as they may be diverting attention away from meaningful reform of school districts and, therefore, they "may, in fact, be inhibiting the development of organizational learning in school systems" (p. 117). Fullan (2005a) has made a similar observation that while "networks are potentially powerful [they] can have their downside" (p. 19): If there are too many of them, they can detract from a clear focus, there may not be any quality control, and they are generally outside of any line-authority; it is therefore unlikely that good ideas would receive the supports needed for implementation. While not commenting directly on networks, Spillane (1996) concluded that districts matter because they influence the implementation of provincial or state-level initiatives either positively or negatively as they engage with schools and school practitioners. In light of this evidence, he concluded that it is "surprising and somewhat troubling ... that school districts have been largely ignored in current school reform proposals" (p. 83).

From our perspective, it is intuitively apparent that it is just plain wrongheaded of policymakers to superimpose additional structures (networks) over preexisting structures (school boards) with the sole purpose of overcoming the weaknesses of the former. Common sense alone dictates that a preferred approach is to focus on reforming the preexisting structures, namely, the school districts. Leithwood, Leonard, and Sharratt (2000) expressed a similar view after having found that teachers in three separate school districts ranked the school district among the top five factors affecting organizational learning processes in schools. They concluded that "rather than eroding or eliminating the functioning of district-level educational organizations, a more defensible policy goal would be to alter the nature of their relationship with schools and to improve their capacities to support professional learning schools" (p. 120).

We share the view that typical school districts are centralized institutionalized bureaucracies that have emphasized top-down command-and-control relationships with schools (Honig, 2006; Walker, 2002). However, it is our view that they mirror the structures and leadership approaches of most other mainstream public and private organizations and, therefore, experience similar challenges of shifting to structures that are conducive to collaborative leadership and organizational learning. We have already established in Chapter 2 that schools experience similar challenges to becoming professional learning communities because of their structures and cultural norms. Therefore, it is clearly naïve to make an assumption that if individual schools are allowed to function as independent agencies, they will miraculously become professional learning communities.

Little and Miller (2007) have observed that "one potential problem with the teacher leadership movement is the presumption that teacher leaders have leadership potential" (p. 145). Having made similar observations as a result of our own work, and having concluded that teacher leadership is essential to organization learning, we conclude that most schools do not have the internal capacity that is required to make the shift to collaborative leadership that is essential to organizational learning without external support. There is growing evidence that school districts can provide the needed support to schools in order for them to overcome the challenges of hierarchy that typically inhibit meaningful reform (Berends, Bodilly, & Kirby, 2002; Clem & Battino, 2006; Datnow, 2005; Elmore, 2002; Fullan, 2005a, 2005b; Green, 2001; Hightower, Knapp, Marsh, & McLaughlin, 2002; Honig, 2003; Leithwood, Leonard, & Sharratt, 2000; McLaughlin & Talbert, 2003; Peterson & Cosner, 2005; Phelps & Addonizio, 2006). For example, after having studied 12 school districts, McLaughlin and Talbert (2003) found strong district effects on the school reform outcomes that include teacher learning community, data-based inquiry, and collaborative problem solving. As a consequence, they have joined "a growing number of researchers and analysts who conclude that, for better or worse, districts matter fundamentally to what goes on in schools and classrooms and that without effective district engagement, school-by-school reform efforts are bound to disappoint" (p. 5). Further, they concluded that supportive school boards functioning as learning organizations are essential to system-wide learning as they "promote and invest in learning through the system—in the central office, in schools, in cross school teacher networks, [and] in units such as the business office that typically are excluded from professional development focused on instruction" (p. 25).

A number of other studies have linked the sustainability of classroom reform to those districts that demonstrate strong commitment to reform initiatives and take measures to ensure that principals provide continued leadership to ensure institutionalization of particular reform initiatives (Klingner, Arguelles, Hughes, & Vaughn, 2001; Vaughn, Klingner, & Hughes, 2000). For instance, in their study of school improvement processes, Huberman and Miles (1984) found that "large-scale, change-bearing innovations lived or died by the amount and quality of assistance that their users received" (p. 273) and that the innovations that were most likely to bring about organizational change appeared to require outside pressure for change and the support of an innovative district. MacGilchrist, Mortimore, Savage, and

Beresford (1995) found similarly that the success of school development planning was largely dependent on the level and quality of the support provided by the school district.

After having reviewed the growing evidence in support of the role of school districts in school reform, Firestone, Mangin, Martinez, and Polovsky (2005) reported that "more recently, analysts have asserted that districts *can* play a key role in supporting instructional reform ... [if they] cope with the numerous pathways through which teaching and learning can be influenced" (p. 414). Similarly, Fullan (2005b) claims that there has been a "shift since 1988 ... from [an emphasis on] single-school, site-based management to district-wide reform, or a situation where all schools in the district are implicated simultaneously" (p. 177). He believes that the evidence is clear that districts can play an essential role in school reform and laments the fact that many jurisdictions have set in play "deliberate strategies from the state level [that] have played down or bypassed the district" (p. 65). It is his contention that such actions are ill founded and that "if you have your systems hat on, you know right away that this is a mistake" (p. 65).

While the evidence in support of school districts as an important agency in the facilitation and sustaining of school and classroom reform has grown over the last decade or so, it must be acknowledged that the continued existence of school districts remains a double-edged sword. Those districts that have been found to have particular characteristics have a positive influence on school reform, while others inhibit reform. For instance, McLaughlin and Talbert (2003) found that

> [a] reforming district ... has a clear theory of change for the system ... [such that] all schools and all elements of the district's policy environment—the business office, human resources, school board, the union and the broader community—are explicitly included in the reform agenda and strategic planning .... Central office administrators and staff are united around a shared vision of improving education for all district students. (pp. 10–11)

Elmore (2000) found that successful districts, in contrast to less-successful districts, place an organizational priority on improving teaching and learning practices rather than viewing teaching and learning as the concern of just individual classroom teachers. In successful districts, he observed a focus on the creation of collaborative leadership and interdependence among constituents in order to capitalize on differences in expertise and to acknowledge the contribution of individuals to collective organizational learning. He concluded that the leadership required for meaningful change must be distributed rather than focused on the exercise of control over certain organizational functions as it is typically described in the management literature. The work of district leaders must be focused primarily on

> enhancing the skills and knowledge of people in the organization, creating a common culture of expectations around the use of those skills and knowledge, holding the various pieces of the organization together in a productive relationship with each other, and holding individuals accountable for their contributions to the collective result. (Elmore, 2000, p. 15)

Minimally, successful school districts share the following characteristics: a shared vision of improving education for each student, an emphasis on individual professional learning, a focus on teaching and learning, collaborative leadership, and system-wide organizational learning (Elmore, 2000; Fullan, 2005a; McLaughlin & Talbert, 2003).

While there exists evidence that school district leadership is essential to the facilitation of successful school districts (Berends et al., 2002; Clem & Battino, 2006; Datnow, 2005; Elliott, 2001; Fullan, 2005a, 2005b; Hightower et al., 2002; Leithwood et al., 2000; Maguire, 2003; Teitel, 2006), and there is growing evidence related to what successful districts look like (Elmore, 2000; Fullan, 2005a, 2005b; McLaughlin & Talbert, 2003), an understanding of how they became successful is sparse (Elmore, 2000; Leithwood, 1995; Leithwood, Louis, Anderson, & Wahlstrom, 2004; Murphy & Hallinger, 2001). Hightower et al. observe that while in the last few years, school districts have moved from being perceived as a bureaucratic backwater of educational policy to being seen as potent sites and sources of educational reform (p. 1), "the majority of districts remain inexperienced with substantive reform" (p. 4). They contend that "we need more powerful frameworks for conceptualizing what a district is and does, how thinking and action from the central office and school board can permeate the teaching environment, and thereby how the district can positively shape the work and careers of its teaching force" (Hightower et al., p. 6). Similarly, Elmore (2000) opined that considering the magnitude of the system-wide expectations imposed on school districts, "there is shockingly little research and documentation of institutional design and practice in exceptionally high performing school districts ... [and furthermore], the knowledge base on which to base advice to local districts on the design of large scale improvement processes is very narrow" (p. 29).

While limited research attention has been given to understanding how school districts become successful, the lack of research attention given to the role of a district superintendent in leading the transformation of a school district from being a traditional hierarchical bureaucratic organization to one that is a professional learning community committed to collaborative leadership is even worse (Hightower et al., 2002; Leavitt, 2003; Leithwood, 1995; Leithwood et al., 2004). Leavitt (2003), for example, observes that while the concept of collaborative leadership is theoretically robust, it has not found its way into mainstream practice of CEOs in our corporations, government, or education. For instance, he recounts problems encountered by Mike, a rookie manager, who did not fully comprehend the reality of the hierarchy. His naïve understanding of the empirically emerging leadership concepts of collaboration, teamwork, and empowerment led him to implement these ideas fully without consideration of the hierarchical context. As a result, he did not remain fully informed of the details of activities that were happening in his area of responsibility. Unfortunately, when he met with his executive committee, they expected him to know the details, and the result for Mike was disastrous. Newton and Tunison (2003) highlight a similar challenge faced by a superintendent who wished to implement a collaborative approach to leadership and organizational learning in a school district:

> Even as school systems are moving toward the implementation of organizational learning, board governance typically remains wedded to traditional notions of control through policy articulation and management through policy implementation. This is an inappropriate model of governance for learning organizations or learning communities .... A school

or school system cannot become a learning organization or a learning community with a governance team that opts out of the learning organization. (p. 2)

Recognizing that top-down models of leadership are the ones most associated with leaders in the public mainstream, and that these models are deeply imbedded into the cultural norms and existing structures of most businesses and public organizations, leads to a better understanding of the challenges associated with leading through a more collaborative, inclusive approach. How does a district superintendent foster collaborative leadership and organizational learning throughout a school district? Hightower et al. (2002) claim that there are few specific images of how to lead successful districts and recommend that these images are best provided through single and comparative case study research. It is toward that purpose that we describe, analyze, and critique the journey of one district superintendent who was committed to collaborative leadership and organizational learning and to the application of the empirical evidence as a means of breaking down the structural, cultural, and micro-political barriers inherent in the traditional hierarchy.

My Voice[1]

Within days of assuming the position of superintendent, my observations and experiences confirmed that the pervasive existing model of leadership in Discovery School District was one of hierarchy where constituents expected the superintendent to be "in sole charge." On one occasion during the first few weeks of my tenure, for example, I failed to provide clarity or direction in response to a question raised by a program specialist. I suggested that the question was one that should be discussed at a meeting of school principals. Being used to top-down decisions, the program specialist assumed that if I did not provide a response, it was because I held no particular view on the matter or I was indecisive, perhaps even "laissez-faire" (an explanation provided by the program specialist when I later questioned his actions), and therefore, he made his own decisions. From this experience, I learned that clarity of intent was essential. While I intended that the program specialist would engage principals in making the particular decision, my deferring a response for that purpose did not mean that he interpreted it that way. The reality, I suspect, was that the program specialist perceived me to be "weak," while many other constituents who received his prescriptive memo likely perceived that district business under the new superintendent would continue to be top-down—business as usual.

During initial one-on-one discussions with each of the three assistant superintendents during the first week of my term as superintendent, my initial impressions were confirmed that the organizational structures and processes were predominantly bureaucratic and hierarchical. It was also apparent that this was an organizational

---

[1] **My Voice** is a recurring section in Chapters 3, 4, 5, and 6 that will provide the thoughts and personal reflections of the superintendent as recorded in his journal or developed through retrospective analysis of documents and recorded events from his five-year journey as a superintendent.

and leadership reality that, for the most part, everyone accepted as "the way things are done around here." Two of the assistant superintendents stressed that the superintendent's office (superintendent and his executive assistant) was set apart from the remainder of the organization, being clearly placed at the apex of the organization as demonstrated through power-over relationships and the symbols of the office. When the superintendent or his executive assistant requested something, everyone understood that it took precedence over all other priorities. As for symbols of power, during special occasions and the holiday season, special recognitions or decorations were distributed in a hierarchical fashion, with the most flamboyant going to the superintendent's office. Similarly, designated parking areas were arranged preferentially according to the hierarchy.

One assistant superintendent was anxious to move forward with a shared decision-making model for the district and was hopeful that it would create a collective focus on student learning. A second assistant superintendent indicated that he preferred to continue to work alone within his zone of authority and essentially viewed collaboration as a waste of time. He believed that organizational learning and collaboration were theoretical constructs that had little merit in practice. He indicated that he had worked at the district level for more than 15 years and that, in his view, the only model that worked was the bureaucratic hierarchical model. He had worked with superintendents who tried to operate using a more collaborative approach to leadership, and the result was disastrous.

A third assistant superintendent confirmed that throughout his entire career of more than 20 years at the district level, and having worked with four previous superintendents, the only model that he knew was hierarchical. While he noted that he was willing to go along with a more participative model of leadership, he was skeptical that it would work. He was anxious, however, to be given more control over his area of responsibility—the board's finances. He expressed real concern for the existing financial circumstances of the board, noting that despite his protests, the board had been overspending and had accumulated a significant deficit. It was necessary to get spending under control and to bring efficiencies to district operations for the benefit of improved educational opportunity for students. In his view, other assistant superintendents, program specialists, and principals did not have the skills or the will to deal with the board's financial crisis. In his experience, the majority of the individuals from each of the aforementioned groups had demonstrated an unwillingness or inability to see budgeting from a systems perspective. Heretofore, at least, they had always been focused on getting a larger portion of the budget for their particular area of responsibility. Consequently, he held the view that strong, decisive leadership would be required in order to bring spending under control.

Informal interviews with school principals, teachers, and support staff and general observations revealed that staff morale was poor and trust levels were very low between management and staff throughout the district. There were dozens of outstanding grievances, and the relationship between management and staff was one of "two solitudes." This was confirmed in a preliminary meeting with union officials for support staff. Union officials stated that they and their members perceived district administrators to be arrogant and inflexible, and they claimed that the school board followed unfair labor practices. They also claimed that the previous superintendent had indicated little interest in support staff issues and that, as a consequence, he had delegated all labor relations responsibilities to other administrative personnel. The assistant superintendent confirmed that he and the comptroller held the delegated responsibility and authority for dealing with support staff and that, essentially, the previous superintendent had few dealings in respect to labor relations.

While support staff and union officials were discontented, it is quite interesting that they appeared not to associate their discontent with the hierarchical structure. As a matter of fact, they were relying on the hierarchy to "fix" their problems as they called upon me as the new superintendent to use my power to change the labor climate. Confirming this view, the assistant superintendent recalled the details of the first meeting between the union president and me in which the union president described the poor labor relations climate in the district. He recalled that the president demanded that I remove him and the comptroller from their labor relations role, claiming that they were the cause of all labor problems in the district. Further, he recalled that the union president was quite disappointed when I indicated that I was willing to work with the union and the current district labor relations personnel to resolve the outstanding grievances, but I was not willing to act unilaterally to deal with outstanding labor issues. The union president became quite agitated and stormed out of the meeting, stating that "labor relations were bad in [this district] and that by the tone of our meeting it seemed as if it were likely to continue that way" (personal communication, November 2006). It was apparent that the union leader expected me to be in charge and to "fix" the labor problems by decree. Both district and union leaders had been approaching labor disputes from a traditional "win-lose, labor versus management" perspective. Any possibility of using a principle-centered, more collaborative approach (Fisher, Ury, & Patton, 1991) to labor relations matters would not likely find favor with either the assistant superintendent and his management staff or union officials. Moreover, the assistant superintendent and the comptroller who had considerable experience and expertise in matters related to arbitration law and collective bargaining advised me against any shift that might indicate to unionized staff that the new superintendent was "soft." They believed any approach other than a "top-down" control model likely would lead to increased labor costs and be detrimental to the overall welfare of the organization.

Hierarchical structures had created an artificial barrier between district office personnel and school personnel as well. Trust levels between school and district-level personnel appeared to be very low, and there existed practically no collaboration among schools or between schools and the district. It appeared that other external groups attributed hierarchical power to the superintendent as well. For example, the Deputy Minister of Education was not happy with the financial state of the board. Within weeks of my appointment she requested that I attend a meeting at which she expected me to present a financial plan for the board that would eliminate the board's deficit. Similarly, within days of my appointment, several parent groups expected me as the new superintendent to resolve issues that previously had not been addressed to their satisfaction. Even though their issues were related to school board decisions, there was an expectation that as superintendent, I would have the authority to revisit those decisions.

Collaborative leadership was not consistent with board norms of practice either (Newton & Tunison, 2003). Board meetings were conducted within the legal framework of the Provincial Schools Act, and proceedings followed *Robert's Rules of Order*. As a result, decisions were made in a win/lose model following the debate of possible solutions put forth as motions that were either approved or rejected. Such a model is contrary to all principles of dialogue and collaboration that are essential to collaborative leadership (Doyle & Straus, 1982). Also, the *Schools Act* required that the superintendent attend all board meetings to provide advice as requested and to respond to questions raised by board trustees. While assistant superintendents were welcomed at meetings, the board expected them to be resource persons for the superintendent whom they perceived to be the only person directly answerable to the board as defined in the *Schools Act*. As superintendent, I was directly accountable to the board while all other employees were accountable to me; therefore, it was understood that I would respond directly to all their questions and that I would be well informed on all issues. This reality became very clear to me at my first board meeting. Several school consolidation initiatives were ongoing at the time, and during my first board meeting, one school consolidation proposal was defeated for the fourth time. At that meeting the board requested that I assume responsibility for restarting and leading a new process to replace the defeated proposal. Bringing successful resolution to school consolidation processes meant careful adherence to a detailed process that had been well defined by legal jurisprudence. Review of the case law in these matters revealed the necessity of a process that was based on public consultations, but dependent on decision-making at the board table through a traditional top-down model of decision-making that reinforced the hierarchy (e.g., Elliott et al. v. Board of Education of Burin Peninsula, 1998a, 1998b; Tracey v. Avalon East School Board, 1998).

Within weeks, I had become convinced that I would not likely succeed, or survive as superintendent, if I did not respect the existing structural and cultural realities of the hierarchy. Shifting to a collaborative approach to leadership that would be facilitative of organizational learning would require much more than a simple announcement or just railing about the inherent flaws of hierarchies and how they "inevitably foster authoritarianism and its destructive offspring: distrust, dishonesty, territoriality, toadying, and fear" (Leavitt, 2003, p. 102). My challenge as superintendent was to effect cultural change. In order to do this, I believed that it was necessary to alter the organizational structures to facilitate collaborative leadership and organizational learning in each school and throughout the district. My critical friends and I recognized, however, this would not be easy when the belief systems and entrenched leadership and organizational norms were those symptomatic of top-down hierarchical bureaucracies.

Having accepted the assumption that leadership success is contingent upon the perceptions of constituents (Lord & Maher, 1990; O'Toole, 1996; Sheppard, 1996), I concluded that organizational learning would occur in the district only if it operated within the reality of the existing hierarchy. Leadership, therefore, had to be focused on reducing the negative impacts of that reality by promoting the collaborative leadership agenda to the limit of the constituents' level of tolerance.

Through the Lens of Critical Friends[2]

We perceived early in our research that district personnel and the school district generally perceived the superintendent in the traditional role at the top of the bureaucratic hierarchy. This had become quite evident during our initial research in project schools. We had also noted in our role as researchers and critical friends that trust was low between the schools and the district office. When our colleague was deciding whether to apply for the position of superintendent, he discussed with us—his research partners—the implications for our research program with the school district. For him, it was an ethical question—he felt it would be unethical of him to be in classrooms and schools if he was also being considered for the position of the superintendent. We agreed, and reluctantly we suspended our research activities until the results of the competition were known. We continued to analyze the data already collected. When he was selected for the position, the wisdom of our withdrawal from research in the district became obvious.

One principal was quite perturbed, fearing that the candid information she had provided us in interviews would influence her career in the future. She let us know that she consulted the teachers' union for advice on how to handle such a situation. In a school meeting, the question of confidentiality in the research we had already conducted was raised by administrators and teachers. They were concerned that the new superintendent had confidential information about them that could be used for evaluation and promotion purposes. Our explanation that our research activities are governed by a code of ethics and that the information we collect can only be used for the purpose it was intended was heard, but people were still uneasy. We argued that although the superintendent had insights from research that he could not delete (like an electronic file), he was a person of integrity and could be trusted.

At this point, our role as researchers in district schools stopped. Although, when invited, we attended district functions as participant-observers, we did not resume an active research role in schools until the superintendent was confident that a culture of trust had been established in the district (about 18 months later). As a result, we did not continue to disseminate findings from our previous research in individual schools as we had previously done because we felt that this might create undue stress upon school principals who might perceive that results reflected negatively upon them. In the interim, while we remained as critical research friends, we pursued a

---

[2] **Through the Lens of Critical Friends** is a recurring section in Chapters 3, 4, 5, and 6 that will provide the critical examination and theoretical analysis of the organizational context and the superintendent's interpretations, actions, and reflections by the two academic researchers acting as critical friends and action researchers.

new direction (at the superintendent's request) and focused our attentions on district administration, governance, and the role of school trustees.

Informal communication with the superintendent and other district personnel, research data, our direct engagement with the school board, and public documents revealed that the pervasiveness of the norms of hierarchy and the school consolidation process proved to be challenging to the superintendent's efforts to lead collaboratively. For instance, our review of district documentation and case law related to the school closure process (Baker v. Burin School District #7, 1999; Elliott et al. v. Board of Education of Burin Peninsula, 1998a, 1998b; Gillingham et al. v. Board of Education of District #3, 1998; Potter v. Halifax Regional School Board, 2001; Tracey v. Avalon East School Board, 1998; Wall v. Corner Brook/Deer Lake/St Barbe District #3, 1998) reveals that, in general, school closure decisions have been a subject of numerous litigations, and therefore, out of necessity, the process is grounded in administrative and legal formalities. The superintendent's role as an advisor to and official spokesperson for the board brought him into the forefront of public discontent related to school closures. School closures were rarely supported by the local population, and often the school board and superintendent were accused of not listening to their public and of making unilateral decisions. Our review of the documentation of public hearings related to school closures revealed that it was common for presenters to direct their frustrations at the superintendent. For instance, one community leader referred to the superintendent as "the emperor with no clothes" and appealed to the board trustees to think for themselves. Given the reality that the school board pursued an agenda of school consolidation throughout the entire five years of our study, it is reasonable to assume that this process would have created an additional challenge to the superintendent's ability to establish credibility and the trust of district constituents that have been highlighted as essential to the facilitation of collaborative leadership and to reducing the toxic derivatives of the hierarchy (Kouzes & Posner, 2003; O'Toole, 1996; Sheppard, 1996).

We observed that the media held a very traditional hierarchical view of leadership as well. The media appeared to hold an underlying assumption that the superintendent had considerable control over board decisions, and the local newspaper frequently published editorials—several written by the editor—that negatively reflected on both the school board and the superintendent. From our vantage point, it appeared that frequently the media sensationalized issues and were supportive of calls to have someone with more authority in the hierarchy, such as the minister of education or the premier, to overrule board decisions with no deference to the *Schools Act 1997* (2005). This reinforced and perpetuated public acceptance of the dominant model of hierarchy in public administration and thereby contributed further to the challenging political climate for the facilitation of a more collaborative approach to leadership.

In sum, at the onset, it was readily apparent that the norms of hierarchical leadership were deeply imbedded into the organizational culture of Discovery School District. The major constituents (principals, employees, parents, government officials, the media, labor unions, etc.) were not well positioned for a shift to collaborative leadership and organizational learning as this would require a rejection of their existing modernistic, micromanaged, and politicized educational organizational paradigm (Giles & Hargreaves, 2006). However, because the superintendent had clearly stated his commitment to establishing a work culture characterized by collaborative leadership and organizational learning during his interview process, the school board was supportive, if not confident, of the prospects for such a shift. It appears to us that if the superintendent had failed to get this support at the point of hiring, in all likelihood he would not have maintained credibility with the school board or other internal or external constituents, and most likely would not have survived in his role as superintendent for any length of time.

References

Anderson, S. (2003). The school district role in educational change: A review of the literature. ICEC working paper #2. Retrieved February 15, 2008 from http://fcis.oise.utoronto.ca/~icec/

Baker v. Burin School District #7 (1999). *Education Law Reporter, 11*(3), 23.

Berends, M., Bodilly, S., & Kirby, S. (2002). Looking back over a decade of whole school reform: The experience of New American Schools. *Phi Delta Kappan, 84*(2), 168–175.

Bogatch, I., & Brooks, C. (1994). Linking school level innovations with an urban school district's central office. *Journal of School Leadership, 4*, 12–27.

Clem, J., & Battino, W. (2006). A systemic change experience in the Chugach School District. *TechTrends, 50*(2), 35.

Chubb, J., & Moe, T. (1990). *Politics, markets and America's schools*. Washington, DC: Brookings Institution.

Datnow, A. (2005). The sustainability of comprehensive school reform models in changing district and state contexts. *Educational Administration Quarterly, 41*(1), 121–153.

Doyle, D., & Finn, C. (1984). American schools and the future of local control. *Public Interest, 77*, 77–95.

Doyle, M., & Straus, M. (1982). *How to make meetings work*. New York: Berkley.

Elliott, R. (2001). *The interaction of district interventions with organizational learning processes in schools and school districts*. Unpublished doctoral dissertation. Toronto, ON: University of Toronto, Canada.

Elliott et al. v. Board Of Education of Burin Peninsula (1998a). *Education Law Reporter, 9*(10), 79.

Elliott et al. v. Board Of Education of Burin Peninsula (1998b). *Education Law Reporter, 10*(3), 25.

Elmore, R. (2000). *Building a new structure for school leadership*. Washington, DC: The Albert Shanker Institute.

Elmore, R. (2002) *Bridging the gap between standards and achievement: The imperative for professional development in education*. Washington, DC: Albert Shanker Institute.

Firestone, W., Mangin, M, Martinez, C., & Polovsky, T. (2005). Leading coherent professional development: A comparison of three school districts. *Educational Administration Quarterly, 41*(3), 413–448.

Fisher, R., Ury, W., & Patton, B. (1991). *Getting to yes: Negotiating agreement without giving in*. Toronto: Penguin.

Fullan, M. (2005a). *Leadership and sustainability*. Thousand Oaks, CA: Corwin.

Fullan, M. (2005b). Turnaround leadership. *The Educational Forum, 69*(2), 174–181.

Giles, C., & Hargreaves, A. (2006). The sustainability of innovative schools as learning organizations and professional learning communities during standardized reform. *Educational Administration Quarterly, 42*(1), 124–156.

Gillingham et al. v. Board of Education of District #3 (1998). *Education Law Reporter, 10*(3), 27.

Green, R. (2001). New paradigms in school relationships: Collaborating to enhance student achievement. *Education, 121*(4), 737.

Hightower, A., Knapp, M., Marsh, J., & McLaughlin, M. (2002). The district role in instructional renewal: Setting the stage for dialogue. In A. Hightower, M. Knapp, J. Marsh, & M. McLaughlin (Eds). *School districts and instructional renewal*. New York: Teachers College.

Honig, M. (2003). Building policy from practice: District central office administrators' roles and capacity for implementing collaborative education policy. *Educational Administration Quarterly. 39*(3), 292–338.

Honig, M. (2006). Street-level bureaucracy revisited: Frontline district central-office administrators as boundary. *Educational Evaluation and Policy Analysis 28*(4), 357–383.

Huberman, M., & Miles, M. (1984). *Innovation up close: How school improvement works*. New York: Plenum.

Klingner, J. K., Arguelles, M. E., Hughes, M. T., & Vaughn, S. (2001). Examining the school wide "spread" of research-based practices. *Learning Disability Quarterly, 24,* 221–234.

Kouzes, J., & Posner, B. (2003). *Credibility*. San Francisco, CA: Jossey-Bass.

Leavitt, H. (2003). Why hierarchies thrive. *Harvard Business Review,* March, 96–102.

Leithwood, K. (1995). Toward a more comprehensive appreciation of effective school district leadership. In K. Leithwood (Ed) *Effective school district leadership: Transforming politics into education* (pp. 315–340). Albany, NY: State University of New York.

Leithwood, K., Leonard, L., Sharratt, L. (2000). Conditions fostering organizational learning in schools. In K. Leithwood (Ed.). *Understanding schools as intelligent systems* (pp. 99–124). Stamford, CT: JAI Press.

Leithwood, K., Louis, K., Anderson, S., & Wahlstrom, K. (2004). *How leadership influences student learning*. The Wallace Foundation. Retrieved November 28, 2005 from http://www.wallacefoundation.org/WF/KnowledgeCenter/KnowledgeTopics/EducationLeadership/HowLeadershipInfluencesStudentLearning.htm

Little, P., & Miller, S. (2007). Hiring the best teachers? Rural values and person-organizational fit theory. *Journal of School Leadership, 17*(2), 118–158.

Lord, R., & Maher, K. (1990). Perceptions of leadership and their implications in organizations. In J. Carroll (Ed.), *Applied social psychology and organizational settings* (pp. 129–154). New Jersey: Lawrence Erlbaum.

MacGilchrist, B., Mortimore, P., Savage, J., & Beresford, C. (1995). *Planning matters: The impact of development planning in primary schools*. London: Paul Chapman.

Maguire, P. (2003). *District practices and student achievement*. Kelowna, BC: Society for the Advancement of Excellence in Education.

McLaughlin, M., & Talbert, J. (2003). *Reforming districts: How districts support school reform*. University of Washington: Center for the Study of Teaching and Policy.

Miller, L. (1984). *American spirit—Visions of a new corporate culture*. New York: William Morrow.

Murphy, J. (2007. June). *Teacher leadership: Barriers and supports*. Paper presented at Teacher Working Conditions that Matter: The Symposium. Toronto, ON, Canada.

Murphy, J., & Hallinger, P. (2001). Characteristics of instructionally effective school districts. *Journal of Educational Research, 81*(3), 175–181.

Newton, P., & Tunison, S. (2003). *Developing policy for learning communities*. Paper presented at the Eighth National Congress on Rural Education, Saskatoon, SK, Canada.

O'Toole, J. (1996). *Leading change*. Toronto: Jossey-Bass.

Peterson, K., & Cosner, S. (2005). Teaching your principal. *Journal of Staff Development, 26*(2), 28–32.

Phelps, J., & Addonizio, M. (2006). How much do schools and districts matter? A production function approach. *Educational Considerations, 33*(2), 51–62.

Potter v. Halifax Regional School Board (2001). *Education Law Reporter, 13*(1), 7.

Rusch, E. (2005). Institutional barriers to organizational learning in school systems: The power of silence. *Educational Administration Quarterly, 41*(1), 83–120.

Schools Act 1997, SNL1997 Chapters-12.2 (2005).

Sheppard, B. (1996). Exploring the transformational nature of instructional leadership. *Alberta Journal of Educational Research, 42*(4), 325–344.

References

Smylie, M., Conley, S., & Marks, H. (2002). Exploring new approaches to teacher leadership for school improvement. In J. Murphy (Ed.), *The educational leadership challenge: Redefining leadership for the 21st century. (101st yearbook of the National Society for the Study of Education, Part L)* (pp. 162–188). Chicago: National Society for the Study of Education.

Spillane, J. (1996). School districts matter: Local educational authorities and state instructional policy. *Educational Policy, 10*(1), 63–87.

Teitel, L. (2006). Supporting school system leaders: The state of effective training programs for school superintendents. The Wallace Foundation. Retrieved March 20, 2006. http://www.wallacefoundation.org/WF/KnowledgeCenter/KnowledgeTopics/EducationLeadership/SupportingSchoolSystemLeaders.htm

Tewel, K. J. (1995). *New schools for a new century*. Delray Beach, FL: St. Lucie Press.

Tracey v. Avalon East School Board (1998). 164 Nfld. & P.E.I.R. 181.

Vaughn, S., Klingner, J. & Hughes, M. (2000). Sustainability of research-based practices. *Exceptional Children, 66*, 163–171.

Walker, E. M. (2002). The politics of school-based management: Understanding the process of devolving authority in urban school districts. *Education Policy Analysis Archives, 10(33)*. Retrieved February 15, 2008 from http://epaa.asu.edu/epaa/

Wall v. Corner Brook/Deer Lake/St Barbe District #3 (1998). *Education Law Reporter, 10*(3), 28.

Chapter 4
Establishing Collaborative Structures

Abstract Establishing structures to facilitate collaborative leadership is essential to the development of a high-performing professional learning community. To enable districts to function in such a manner, the first step is to identify the structures that inhibit it and to replace them with facilitating ones. In this chapter we draw from the research literature on collaborative leadership and organizational learning, our own research in schools, and the experiences of a superintendent and two university critical friends to document how this occurred in one school district. This work shows that while the implementation of collaborative structures that are facilitative of a collaborative approach to leadership and organizational learning throughout a school district is complex and full of risks, it can be achieved if deliberately championed by a leader committed to engaging others in the process.

Collaboration that is essential to organizational learning is closely aligned with Senge's (1990) learning organization discipline of team learning and is focused on the importance of teachers building "collaborative work cultures inside and outside the school ... [and] assuming direct responsibility for changing the norms and practices of the entire school" (Fullan, 1995, p. 233). It is based on the assumption that "in the right atmosphere, people will contribute and make commitments because they want to learn, to do good work for its own sake, and to be recognized as people" (Senge, Roberts, Ross, Smith, & Kleiner, 1994, p. 200). In order to create this right atmosphere, it is essential that a leader consider the fundamental values and perspectives of followers and demonstrate respect for them by "always practice[ing] the art of inclusion" (O'Toole, 1996, p. 37). Senge et al. suggest genuine collaboration will occur only through dialogue, and Freire (2004) contends that dialogue can occur only when equality exists. Schein (1993) opines that if organizational learning is to occur, dialoguing must take place both at the executive level and across all levels of an organization:

> Organizational learning is not possible unless some learning first takes place in the executive subculture ... Such self analysis will inevitably involve periods of dialogue .... Dialogue at the executive level is not enough for organizational learning to occur, [however]. The process of communicating across the hierarchical levels of an organization will require further dialogue because of the likelihood that different strata operate with different assumptions. (p. 50)

Through dialogue, constituents are able to move beyond the advocacy of particular perspectives, thereby allowing them to engage in double-loop learning as they examine one another's mental models (Argyris, 1982; Senge, 1990; Senge et al., 1994). Double-loop learning refers to learning that is generative and transformational in nature, where the focus is on adjusting overall rules and norms rather than specific activities or behaviors. It occurs when, in addition to detection and correction of errors (single-loop learning), the organization questions its basic assumptions to find out why the problem occurred in the first place. Duffy (2003) highlights the importance of dialogue as a means of enabling double-loop learning:

> People often are unaware of their mental models and their effects, yet these models determine what people pay attention to and therefore influence what people do and how they do it. Left unexamined and unchallenged, mental models influence people to see what they have always seen, do what they have always done, be what they have always been, and therefore produce the same results. Mental models can be roadblocks to systemic school improvement or extraordinary supports for systemic, district wide change. Helping educators and school systems surface, examine, evaluate, and change their personal and organizational mental models is a key step in creating and sustaining systemic school improvement. (p. 36)

Rusch (2005) recognizes the importance of collaborative dialogue to organizational learning in school systems as well, concluding that organizational learning is "dependent on members developing strategies to communicate honestly and to give feedback about issues that are institutionally taken for granted" (p. 90). Similarly, Green and Etheridge (2001) concluded from their investigation of 11 effective school districts that their effectiveness appeared to be largely dependent on collaborative structures and processes that facilitated dialogue, which in turn contributed to the development of common beliefs and shared visions.

Unfortunately, few schools or school systems have the leadership capacity to facilitate the creation of collaborative structures that will facilitate dialogue and professional learning. Barth (2001) contends that in spite of the rhetoric in respect to collaboration and shared decision-making, many schools remain in a parallel play pattern, whereby the interactions between teachers and the principal are plagued by suspicion and acrimony and teachers are guarded and adversarial toward both school and district administrators. Such conditions have been identified as typical negative side effects of the traditional bureaucratic hierarchy (Leavitt, 2003). In schools, the traditional structure has overburdened principals and de-professionalized teachers. School principals are just too busy with daily routines to engage in a meaningful leadership role. Their work environment is composed of an enormous number of brief tasks that are complex, varied, and demanding, leaving little time for principals to focus on developing the school as a professional learning community (Mintzberg, 1973; Peterson, 1982; Peterson & Cosner, 2005). Further exacerbating the intense pace of the typical workday of a school principal, some academics and administrators who are firmly committed to the "power-over" model of hierarchy have proposed that principals must assume a prescriptive narrowly defined inspectorial instructional leadership role. (See Sheppard, 1996, for a more detailed discussion of narrowly defined instructional leadership.)

As for the limiting nature of the district bureaucracy, we have documented in Chapter 3 that multiple studies have found that most school districts function as traditional hierarchical bureaucracies and consequently present themselves as major inhibitors of school-level dialoguing and problem solving that are essential to the facilitation of "system-level restructuring or cross-system organizational learning" (Rusch, 2005, p. 87). It is evident that while the building of leadership capacity in schools and school districts through the broad-based participation of various constituent groups as collaborative leaders as a means to school improvement has widespread theoretical and empirical support, the most typical organizational structures in schools and school districts continue to be bureaucratic and hierarchical (e.g., Argyris, 1999; Lambert, 2005; Sheppard & Brown, 2006). The challenge, then, is how to get from "here to there!" Simply stating that an organization is going to be collaborative and that leadership will be distributed will most likely result in failure (Sheppard, 2003).

Argyris (1999) has observed that while "there is a revolution brewing in the introduction of new organizational forms to complement or to replace the more traditional pyramidal form" (p. 107), the conditions necessary for the successful implementation of these new forms "are difficult to create" (p. 108). Shifting to a collaborative approach to leadership and facilitating an environment in which constituents feel genuinely invited to engage in leadership and are willing to do so are not processes that occur automatically as a result of decree or by merely providing the opportunity. Rusch (2005) recognizes this reality as well, as she cautions that simply increasing opportunity for collaborative learning is not enough.

Having defined high-capacity schools as "learning communities that amplify leadership for all, learning for all, [and] success for all" (p. 40), Lambert (2005) laments the limitations imposed by the pervasiveness of current structures and concludes that just announcing that a school or district is going to adopt a collaborative approach to leadership is unlikely to result in meaningful change. She contends that attention must be given to creating structures through which such participation can occur. This is a view that is shared by Sparks (2005), who has observed that structural change, while not sufficient to bring about meaningful change in schools, is almost always required.

In order to shift to a more collaborative leadership approach, a logical first step is to identify the structures that inhibit it and to replace them with facilitating ones (Sheppard & Brown, 2007). However, such a change is much more complex than simply making adjustments to an organizational chart (Barth, 1990; Dufour & Eaker, 1998; Schlechty, 1997). In addition to the direct limiting control of traditional district structures, constituents' mental models are influenced by "a school district's social architecture ..., what people think their school district stands for and how they think it should function" (Duffy, 2003, p. 31). This limits the constituents' capacity to engage in meaningful dialogue, their willingness to challenge the status quo, and their ability to accommodate new and innovative ideas (Duffy, 2003; Sparks, 2005). Consequently, while it is important to make structural changes that signal to constituents that the district and in particular its superintendent is committed to a collaborative approach of leadership and organizational learning, the changes have to remain within the constituents' level of tolerance for change (O'Toole, 1996) and must be focused on altering the organizational mental models that comprise the social architecture.

My Voice

Nurturing Collaborative Leadership at Discovery School District

Given the hierarchical nature of the existing structures and the general acceptance of the hierarchy by the various constituents and formal leaders, it is not surprising that there were few examples of collaborative leadership in Discovery School District. As noted in Chapter 3, within the first month of my term as superintendent, I observed that Barth's (2001) parallel play existed not only at the school level as he had described, but at the district level as well. For instance, while school principals and program specialists knew and spoke the language of collaboration and team leadership, there was very little evidence of it being practiced. It appeared to me that each played a competitive game of one-upmanship with the other and that this was particularly pronounced among school principals.

The model of leadership at the school level was also very traditional, with a few exceptions. Given that the school principal was the primary communication link between the district and school personnel, this presented a significant challenge to shifting the model from a traditional bureaucracy to a professional learning community where teachers considered themselves to be leaders. While several schools had been engaged in an organizational learning partnership initiative with us as university critical friends, this initiative was viewed only as another project that might have some implications for school development. Certainly, it was not viewed as having implications for how the district was led or administered. Prior to my assuming the role of superintendent, it became painfully clear to my research colleague and me that our organizational learning research and development project was unlikely to have much impact on any of the non-project schools or the district as a whole without a deliberate district-wide effort directed at altering structures and modifying leadership approaches (Berends, Bodilly, & Kirby, 2002; Clem & Battino, 2006; Datnow, 2005; Firestone, Mangin, Martinez, & Polovsky, 2005; Fullan, 2005; Hall & Hord, 2006; Honig, 2003; Leithwood, Leonard, & Sharratt, 2000).

While I recognized the need for the district to move toward more collaborative approaches to leadership, I struggled somewhat with how to approach the initiation of change in that direction. Attempting to employ a leadership approach that was not within the accepted tolerance levels of the existing "mental models" of the majority of the organization's constituents would not likely be successful. However, subordinating my perspectives to those held by others and adopting the most common leadership practices to please them would not be leadership. On this matter, I was guided by the work of O'Toole (1996) and of Kouzes and Posner (2003). O'Toole (1996) cautioned that while a leader must consider the fundamental values and perspectives of followers, he/she must avoid "the too common political practice of pandering to the base wishes of the lowest common denominator—promising whatever the masses think they want" (pp. 9–10). A leader must constantly test the limit of public tolerance for change that will inevitably involve trial and error as the limit is pushed beyond that which is acceptable. But the essential value throughout this process must be respect for people (O'Toole, 1996). Similarly, while Kouzes and Posner (2003) emphasized the importance of connecting with constituents, they concluded as well that a leader must have a "clear sense of direction [and] sometimes ... should listen to [his/her] conscience and ... intuition, instead of [his/her] constituents" (p. 269).

Having made the decision to move forward, the next step, I thought, would be to communicate my vision of leadership for the district and my desire to implement a more collaborative leadership approach that would engage school personnel in district-level decision-making, but once again, that appeared to me to be a paradox. I would be using my position power within the existing hierarchy to impose on others my vision of a more collaborative, inclusive approach to leadership and decision-making while emphasizing the importance of developing a shared vision. On the other hand, I was aware of the finding by Bodilly, Keltner, Purnell, Reichardt, and Schuyler (1998) that "school staff were clear and forceful" (p. 88) in articulating that district leaders must clearly communicate the importance of any new effort and therefore the level of priority it should be given by leadership actions. Additionally, I was aware that moving away from dependence on hierarchical leadership and its supporting bureaucratic structures that were grounded in "deep beliefs and assumptions" (Senge et al., 1994) would involve constituents unlearning the old ways of doing prior to their being able to think and interact in new ways. Such a shift would require a period of years and "for a long time it [might] appear that there [was] nothing going on ... as people talk[ed] about new ideas ... practice[d] the application of [new approaches and] ... design[ed] and implement[ed] changes in infrastructure" (p. 44). This lengthy, complex process would not likely occur unless constituents had a clear and compelling vision of the organization that we were striving toward; therefore, it appeared essential that I share my personal vision for the organization (Bass & Riggio, 2006). Otherwise, my efforts to promote collaborative leadership throughout the district might lead to perceptions that I was merely participative or, even worse, that I was a laissez-faire leader.

In light of this apparent paradox and my self-doubt, I consulted my administrative colleagues in the school district and dialogued with my critical friends as to the correct course of action. Collectively, we concluded that it was essential to introduce my desired shift in leadership approach "with sufficient drama and flair that people [would] believe things [were] going to change" (Schlechty, 1990, p. 134). As a result of these consultations, my self-doubt was diminished, and I articulated my vision of leadership (see Fig. 4.1 for an outline of this vision) to multiple constituents commencing the second week following my assuming the position as superintendent. My intent was to provide a clear, compelling articulation of the moral purpose of education in the district that was to improve learning for each student and to outline the benefits of developing a culture of collaborative leadership that I believed was

---

The Superintendent of Education

- must pour his heart into his work.
- must attend to the culture of the District.
- must be guided by such a philosophy of leadership that is rooted in respect for people.
- must be collaborative and very much dependent on the collective wisdom of students, staff, trustees, schools councils, and other educational stakeholders.
- must understand and be able to lead a successful strategic planning process that will allow us to develop cultures of learning that allow traditional barriers to growth to be replaced with cultures of openness and trust that facilitate growth.
- must be a champion of positive change that will bring us closer to a shared identity and a shared vision of the future, as we hold on to the strengths of our diversity and our valued traditions.
- must ensure that the district's constituents have an opportunity to develop shared images of the future they wish to create.
- must ensure that the district is student focused.
- must foster an environment that will ensure that we continue to explore and develop innovative programs.
- must be committed to the meaningful engagement of all constituent groups in the leadership process.
- must be a proactive communicator who will be a strong representative voice for education generally, and for the District in particular.
- must foster a culture of collaboration and a spirit of ownership among students and staff so that they are proud of their association with this District.
- should foster the development of systems thinking.
- must be aware and interested in the activities of individual employees and provide encouragement and support. This interest, encouragement, and support must be given for personal issues as well as for job-related issues.
- must be a strong advocate providing educational opportunity for all students in respect to the provincially articulated foci: Aesthetic Expression, Citizenship, Communication, Personal Development, Problem Solving, and Technical Competence.
- is responsible to the School Board for the supervision and administration of programs, budget, and all activities of the District within the law as set out by the Schools Act and the School Board By-Laws.
- is a senior administrator within the k-12 system within the province and must contribute to the leadership of that system.

Fig. 4.1 Superintendent's leadership vision (outline)

required if this purpose were to be realized. This presentation signaled expectations that constituents should have of the superintendent, and at the same time, it set out clear expectations for other district and school leaders and opened the door for collaboration.

Just announcing the vision without a strategy for implementation, however, would result in little or no change (Hall & Hord, 2006). Following the articulation of my vision of leadership in the district, the next step was to build support at the administrative and school board levels to begin the implementation process. With this support, I could begin altering structures and introducing the theoretical frameworks, strategies, and methods that would allow us to overcome the "dysfunctionalities of traditional hierarchical and bureaucratic structures" (Murphy, 2007, p. 2) and would facilitate our becoming a professional learning community where collaborative leadership and organizational learning would be the accepted norm in individual schools and throughout the school district (York-Barr & Duke, 2004). The steps included were as follows: setting up administrative structures in support of collaborative leadership, facilitating a collaborative culture and shared decision-making, developing a commitment to a shared vision of teaching and learning, redesigning personal professional learning in a caring inclusive culture of high expectations, redefining school improvement and strategic planning as strategic thinking and adaptive learning, and developing a new strategic plan.

In the revised structure (see Fig. 4.2), the Administrative Council would meet one day per week, rather than twice per month as was the past practice, and decisions were to be made by consensus. In addition to that, I sought Administrative Council support to shift greater decision-making authority to school personnel and to engage them in district-level decision-making. Both the Advisory Council and Principals' Meetings were replaced by a General Administrative Council (GAC) that would have decision-making authority within the district. Members of GAC included all principals, program specialists, assistant superintendents, the comptroller, the human resources administrator, and the superintendent. This group of approximately 60 members met in six-week intervals and as priorities dictated (approximately 10 meetings a year) to engage in dialogue and decision-making around key issues in education (GAC meeting minutes, 2000–2004). GAC meeting agendas were planned

School District Organizational Structure

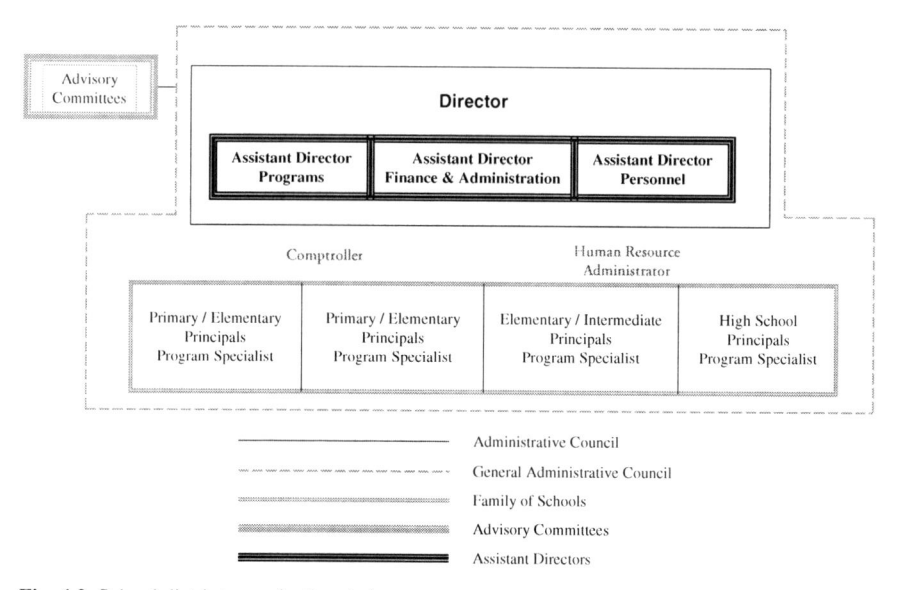

Fig. 4.2 School district organizational chart

by a smaller group, the General Administrative Council Planning (GACP) committee, which was composed of GAC members who were the representatives of each GAC constituency selected for a one-year term by their colleagues. As superintendent, I was to be a permanent member of this group.

In order to facilitate collaboration and shared decision-making, GAC was composed of four clusters of schools of similar grade levels referred to as Families of Schools. These Families of Schools were responsible for teaching and learning, school development, and school councils.[1] Each GAC member belonged to one Family, and the individual Families became the primary operating units for dialogue at GAC meetings as a necessary precursor to collaborative decision-making. Beyond formal GAC meetings, the Families of Schools provided the mechanism through which principals, teachers, and other school employees became engaged in across-school leadership and shared decision-making as they planned learning events, engaged in school development, and learned together. Each Family was facilitated by a program specialist who would be a "district champion" for these schools and who would act as brokers and boundary spanners between the schools within each Family, across Families of Schools, and between schools and the district office (Swinnerton, 2007; Wenger, 1998).

As a result of these additional responsibilities assigned to program specialists, it was necessary to redefine their role. Their previously existing responsibilities inhibited meaningful collaboration because each program specialist had been assigned a specific and unique role focused primarily on subject specialization. The assistant superintendent of programs and I discussed with the program specialists team our desire to foster more collaboration and sought their input in a revised model. While there was some resistance among the program specialists to a role change, most participated in a dialogue (early use as opposed to an ideal form) that led to a revised role based on a mirror image–plus approach (Galbraith & Lawler, 1993). In the mirror-image role, each program specialist had responsibilities that were similar to others in respect to their specific Family of Schools and their broker and boundary spanning roles. As noted above, they were "district champions" for their schools. In the plus role, each program specialist maintained his/her previously existing unique role with district-wide responsibilities for an area of specialization (e.g., physical education, literacy, mathematics) (see Fig. 4.3).

In addition to their involvement as members of GAC, program specialists continued to meet biweekly with the assistant superintendent of programs. In the revised model, decision-making at program specialists' meetings was to occur through dialogue and consensus-building processes, and they could no longer make unilateral decisions regarding programs and teacher professional development. Their level of engagement in those decisions would be determined by GAC.

---

[1] A school council is a democratically elected advisory group consisting of parents, community representatives, students, teachers, and the school principal whose purpose is to develop, encourage, and promote policies, practices, and activities to enhance the quality of school programs and the levels of student achievement in a school.

> All Program Specialists in the district will assume duties within a Mirror Image–Plus Framework. In the mirror-image role, each program specialist has responsibilities that are similar to others. In the mirror-plus role, each program specialist has a specific assigned role that differs from others.
>
> *Mirror Image*
> All program specialists are responsible for school development in a Family of Schools for the assigned level (Primary/Elementary or Intermediate-Senior High). Responsibilities include school development planning, teaching and learning, student assessment, personal & professional growth & development, teacher hiring, school reports, and school councils.
>   Within the above-noted areas of responsibilities, they are expected to engage in decision-making, liaison, consultation, planning, and action.
>
> *Mirror Plus*
> Each program specialist has a specific responsibility for the programs and personnel directly associated with the area of specialization (Active, Healthy Living, Literacy, French, etc.) for k-12. As a result of this Mirror-Plus role, for example, Program Specialists for Student Support will support and coordinate the work of itinerant teachers; provide training and support to teachers, principals, and other program specialists in Pathways planning, and in the development of Individual Student Support Plans; and monitor the delivery of programming to all students with diagnosed exceptionalities. The Program Specialist for a specific subject area or field of specialization (mathematics, physical education, literacy, visual, and performing arts, etc.) will support and coordinate work of teachers of that specialization and will monitor all programming for instruction in that subject area or field, including student course selection, teaching methodologies, accomplishment of curriculum objectives across grade levels, student assessment strategies, and student achievement levels on school, district, and provincial tests and examinations.

Fig. 4.3 Mirror image–plus framework for program specialists
Source: Discovery School District Handbook on Administrative Structures.

Collaboratively Defining Shared Decision-Making

Principals, teachers, support staff, program specialists, and other district-level personnel had heard superintendents make commitments related to shared decision-making before, but it had not materialized. Similar to other jurisdictions, the words had been articulated often and promises had been made, but in practice, they had experienced a continuation of the traditional models of top-down management where decisions were made through a hierarchical system of power and authority based on formal organizational roles (Bimber, 1994; Dunlap & Goldman, 1991; Hansen & Roza, 2005). I observed that they were quite cynical of any mention of terms like empowerment and shared decision-making. Many expressed the view that most of their colleagues believed that it was just another case of downloading of responsibility and increased accountability, while those at the top made all the important decisions. While the new administrative structures and changing roles facilitated shared decision-making at GAC, it was just an initial step. The next step was to collaboratively define decision-making for the school district.

  I believed that the Wynn and Guiditus (1984) approach of developing shared decision-making matrices would overcome the existing cynicism as it would clearly define the powers and rights of the various groups and individuals in respect to decision-making (see Fig. 4.4). After having received the support of the Administrative Council and the GACP committee for this idea, I introduced it to GAC who decided that as an initial step, two decision-making matrices would be developed: (1) teaching and learning and (2) repair and maintenance. Because the issue of repair and maintenance had been a constant source of tension between district and school personnel, and because it was deemed to be the least complex of the two, GAC agreed to begin with that issue.

As the process began, I observed quickly that the interpretation of the GAC membership of shared decision-making was influenced by varied mental models. For the majority, it meant that if principals were to be part of a shared decision-making process, then no decisions would get made without the agreement of the entire group. For many, the general interpretation of the term consensus was simple: Everyone agrees, or no decision can be taken! Moreover, early discussions at GAC convinced me that some members were of the view that the shared decision-making process would apply to all decisions irrespective of legal or financial requirements or government or school board bylaws, policies, or regulations. It was obvious that if shared decision-making were to be a possibility, clarity was required around the understanding of the superintendent's legal and fiduciary obligations and the concepts of shared decision-making and consensus building. Without clarity in respect to shared decision-making and consensus building, it was most likely that decision-making would become time consuming and costly. Few decisions would get made, and learning in the organization would be inhibited. As for my legal and fiduciary responsibilities, it would have been foolish and irresponsible of me to have abandoned all constraints (Kouzes & Posner, 2003). I was constrained by government, the school board, parents, students, employees, members of the public, the economic system, and a multitude of unforeseen forces.

I recommended that the matrices be developed through consensus decision-making that would be guided by the Interaction Method (Doyle & Straus, 1982) and strategies, tools, and methods outlined in the *Fifth Discipline Fieldbook* (Senge et al., 1994). The consensus process that was to be adopted would ensure an efficient reconciliation of value choices, rather than some open concept that was understood as everyone's first choice. To that end, consensus was defined as "the judgment arrived at by most of those concerned" (*Merriam-Webster* online). It was understood to be

Rights	Powers
I Right to be informed	1. Power to decide and act alone
	2. Power to decide and act but must inform
V Right to veto or amend	3. Power to decide but subject to veto or amendment before acting
A Right to advise	4. Power to decide but meet and discuss before acting (must have someone with Advise rights, but may or may not have someone with Veto rights)

Fig. 4.4 Decision-making rights and powers

a condition in which everyone is willing to go along without sabotaging a decision. While a particular decision may not be the first choice for all members, each individual has had sufficient opportunity to influence others to his/her point of view and has heard what a large majority in the group believe is the correct decision and can accept it without feeling that he/she will lose anything important. As a result, all understand the issue, and it has enough support to have a good chance for success (adapted from Doyle & Straus, 1992). (GAC minutes, November 2000)

Also, to ensure a process that would allow me to deliver on my administrative, legal, and fiduciary obligations as superintendent, I highlighted the right of veto that was available to all GAC members within the consensus process. Within our definition, consensus was considered to have been reached when each individual was able to accept the collective decision without feeling that he/she would lose anything important. Essentially, this gave veto power to each individual including the superintendent. For my part, I emphasized that my veto power would be restricted to any decision that might specifically compromise my obligations as noted above and that my use of veto would be accompanied by a detailed explanation. Without the articulation of this understanding at the outset, my veto of the group's decisions would likely have resulted in serious misunderstandings and a loss of trust in the entire shared decision-making process.

Each of the decision-making matrices was subject to ongoing monitoring by two teams (one team for each matrix) appointed by GAC. These monitoring teams were responsible for the implementation of each of the two matrices: seeking feedback from GAC members regarding any perceived deficiencies and recommending to GAC any proposed changes.

The process of developing the Repair and Maintenance Matrix proved to be an excellent introduction to shared decision-making. It provided opportunity for GAC members (1) to practice dialoging as they engaged in identifying the repair and maintenance issues and the systems interactions that influence decision-making in this area and (2) to learn about and practice consensus-building strategies as they made decisions about the level of power and the rights that were most appropriate for each of the groups and individuals who were included in the matrix. While the initial steps were challenging and there were many skeptics and naysayers, the group persevered and successfully completed a Repair and Maintenance Matrix. Successful completion of the first process convinced GAC members that this could be practical and useful in decision-making.

The development of the second matrix was much more complex as might have been expected, given that it dealt with teaching and learning (see Fig. 4.5 to view an excerpt of this matrix). While the first matrix was developed within a four-month time span, the development of Teaching and Learning Matrix continued for 14 months. The task of GAC was to brainstorm and reach consensus on all factors that impacted teaching and learning, to categorize the factors, and then to reach consensus on rights and powers related to each category. As part of this process, principals were asked to take the preliminary matrix to their teaching staff for further

Issues	Superintendent	AS Finance	AS Personnel	AS Programs	Admin. Council	GAC	Family of Schools	Principals	Program Specialists	Comptroller	HR Administrator
Matrix development	V	A	A	V	V	3					
Professional development											
School growth and development plans	V4		A4	A4	V4		A	V4	A4		
New models of staff development	V4		V4	V4	V4		A	A4	A4		1
Teacher collaboration	V4		V4	V4			A	A4	A4		
Self-evaluation/reflection on instructional practice	V4		A4	A4				A4	A4		
Teacher growth and development plans	V4		V4	A4				A4	A4		
Connections within and among schols	V4		A4	A4			1	4	A4		
Teacher training (preservice and in-service)	V4		A4	A4				A4	A4		
Program implementation	V4		A4	V4	V4		1	A4	A4		

Fig. 4.5 Excerpt of decision-making matrix: Teaching and learning

development because this matrix, when developed, would guide decision-making for all identified aspects related to teaching and learning at the school level.

The process of developing the matrices helped overcome the skepticism related to the district administrators' commitment to shared decision-making. GAC members recognized that the traditional power holders (the administrative team and the superintendent) had engaged in a collaborative process in which within clearly defined parameters all voices were given equal weight. They recognized my administrative, fiduciary, and legal responsibilities and accepted the necessity of recognizing veto power as a safeguard that must be built into the matrix-building process. In practice, the veto power afforded to individual group members was not employed throughout the entire process of matrices development (confirmed through a review of GAC minutes and interviews with various GAC members), but it appears that its inclusion in the process may have served as a reminder of organizational accountabilities for all. As a result of the newly created GAC structure and the development of the shared decision-making matrices, school principals and their teachers and support staff that had heretofore been cut out of the district decision-making processes contributed to the development of the district-level matrices that in turn clearly defined their powers at the local school level. These were important first steps in building a collaborative culture.

The process was very time consuming, and I often wondered to myself about the utility of the process. However, as I reflected on the matrix development process, I was reminded of Fullan's (1993) book *Change Forces*, where he identifies eight basic lessons of a new change paradigm. In Lesson 4 he notes that under the conditions of dynamic complexity, one needs a good deal of reflective experience before one can form a plausible vision, and that a shared vision, which is essential for success, must evolve through the dynamic interaction of organizational members and leaders. Vision, he claims, "emerges from, more than it precedes, action" (p. 28). Similar to my own experience, he concludes by stating that this process takes time, and because it is an open-ended and authentic process, it avoids premature formulation of a vision. I was experiencing this very phenomenon in action, and in fact, the vision was reshaped many times to accommodate the complexities of change. Also, collective ownership for the process and the product happened because of the learning that occurred from engagement in the development process.

Through the Lens of Critical Friends

Analysis of the Structural Changes

The structural changes that included the creation of GAC and the Families of Schools were designed to facilitate the needed district-wide engagement of teachers, support staff, principals, program specialists, and district administrators as collaborative leaders and decision-makers in order to support the district goal of organizational learning and capacity building. It created conditions that both necessitated and facilitated the co-creation of the shared decision-making matrices that defined clearly the interaction between the district and schools and moved much of the decision-making authority from district-level personnel to GAC members. Through engagement in collaborative processes at GAC, members learned about and experienced models of collaboration that stimulated them to challenge their existing mental models of hierarchical leadership. It became a practice field and safe haven for principals to develop new skills, capacities, and practices essential to the development of their schools as learning communities and equipped them to "engage teachers [in their own schools] in problem solving rather than render them helpless through directives and granting or withholding permission" (Lambert, 2005, p. 40). Furthermore, it provided a forum through which principals could act as boundary spanners and brokers between constituents in their individual schools, other schools, and the district office.

The creation of GAC and the Families of Schools and of a shared decision-making matrix in teaching and learning, however, resulted in considerable unease for program specialists (Program Division meeting minutes, 2000–2002). Some perceived the elimination of the Advisory Council and the granting of decision-making authority to principals in respect to teaching and learning through GAC to be an erosion of their power (program specialist Susan, personal communications, April 2006). Moreover, many expressed their unease with their redefined mirror image–plus role and requested the superintendent's attendance at several Program Division meetings to address those concerns. It appears, however, that over the course of a two-year period through participation in GAC and various dialogue sessions with the superintendent and as a result of positive experiences as champions of their School Families, they entered into a stage of routine use (Hall & Hord, 2006) and began to view their new role as members of a collaborative leadership team as improved practice. One program specialist (personal communications, January 2007) commented that "despite the original skepticism, the team of program specialists had come to realize that they had become effective champions of professional learning in each Family." Even more compelling evidence of their growing comfort level with their new role is the fact that given the opportunity to discuss their work with a minister of education four years after they had adopted the mirror-image/mirror image–plus role, they presented it as a model for all other districts (the acting assistant superintendent of programs, personal communication, April 2004).

The need to build capacity at the school level and to include teachers as partners in educational reform has been well documented (Fullan, 2001; Hall & Hord, 2006; Hargreaves & Evans, 1997; Harris, 2005; Leithwood, Louis, Anderson, & Wahlstrom, 2004; Silins & Mulford, 2002). Hall and Hord (2006) contend that organizations are composed of individuals and learn only as individuals learn. Consequently, while many change processes can be directed at various groups, in final analysis, it must be recognized that "successful change starts and ends at the individual level" (Hall & Hord, 2006, p. 7). Prior to the creation of GAC and Families of Schools, there was practically no across-school knowledge sharing other than the inclusion of teachers or support staff on various ad hoc district committees. This was particularly limiting for teachers in smaller schools where there was only one teacher per grade level or subject area specialty. Also, there was no opportunity for teachers to influence district decisions. The district norm for interactions among schools was one of competition and one-upmanship, rather than of collaboration. "Schools [were] ... terrible at learning from each other" (Fullan, 2001, p. 92); therefore, capacity building was limited. The learning network that was created and the capacity that was built through the GAC and the Families of Schools contributed significantly to collaborative leadership and the facilitation of district-wide learning. As capacity grew within the district, not only did the schools within each Family work together, but they included schools from other Families (referred to by Family members as their cousins). The following comment by one GAC member is indicative of the growth in collaborative leadership that occurred over a period of four years:

> I remember people sitting [in Families of Schools at GAC] and wondering what we were doing here. Then at the end, they would see it. We built more capacity for learning and growth [and] we built leadership .... I really saw that, at the time when [one of our school principals] received the award for Outstanding Principal of the Year from the Canadian Association of Principals. All the principals from our district felt like they were one ..., and that happened because of what we had achieved together, as one. (Personal Communication, March 2007)

The shift in the level of collaboration throughout the district was dramatic enough to be noticed by some school board members as well. One board member, for example, stated that she was quite impressed that all school district administrative personnel and all school principals now met monthly to make district-wide decisions. She attributed the creation of GAC and the increase in collaborative decision-making to the superintendent's collaborative approach to leadership. Overall, it appears that GAC and the Families of Schools implementation facilitated the development of a critical mass of leaders who ceased to operate as individuals within a narrow span of authority and began "to think in bigger terms and to act in ways that affect[ed] larger parts of the [district] as a whole" (Fullan, 2005, p. 27).

The development of shared decision-making matrices contributed considerably to the effectiveness of the new structures as it provided the context and practice field for initial efforts at collaborative decision-making and in the final analysis clearly defined shared decision-making in critical areas of decision-making that frequently create conflict between schools and districts. After having observed various shared decision-making and site-based management initiatives, Bimber (1994) concluded that most were unsuccessful in bringing about school reform because, years after they were introduced, decision-making related to essential governance issues had not been shared with school personnel. He concluded that "to be effective at removing constraints and creating environments in which schools take responsibility for the education process, decentralization should address the need for comprehensive changes across all interrelated categories of decision-making" (p. ix). It appears that the creation of GAC and the development of shared decision matrices contributed greatly to the accomplishment of that objective in Discovery School District.

Aside from the intended specific benefit of developing clarity around decision-making related to teaching and learning and school repair and maintenance, the development of the Teaching and Learning Matrix brought a focus on teaching and learning that led to the development of a district-wide shared vision for teaching and learning (more on this in Chapter 5). An unanticipated benefit of both matrix development processes was the apparent enhancement of the superintendent's credibility among GAC members. While developing the matrices, GAC members called upon the superintendent on several occasions to lead the group forward. Several GAC members noted that during the process the superintendent demonstrated considerable tolerance of ambiguity and an ability to resolve conflicts. As a consequence, they attributed the successful completion of the task to his leadership (assistant superintendent of personnel, personal communication, October 2003). This may have led to enhancement of his leadership credibility (Gardner, 1990; Kouzes & Posner, 2003). Gardner (1990) has argued, for example, that "A loyal constituency is won when the people conscientiously or unconscientiously, judge the leader to be capable of solving their problems and meeting their needs" (p. 28). A third related benefit is that it contributed positively to the level of trust among GAC members. Because the building of the matrices was an iterative problem-solving process, trust that is essential to a collaborative approach to leadership (Bryk & Schneider, 2003; Tschannen-Moran & Hoy, 2000) was developed as people observed that administrative council members did not pretend to have all the answers and that they were interested in learning from and with others.

Teacher Perceptions of Collaboration

While there existed convincing qualitative evidence that collaborative structures were established at the district level that were inclusive of those with formal leadership roles in schools and at district office, we were interested in finding out the extent to which other constituents such as school board trustees and school-level personnel (teachers and support staff) perceived that leadership was a team effort, that structures existed to encourage them to collaborate, and that decision-making was shared. Toward that purpose, we completed interviews with school board trustees and collected survey data from school personnel (primarily teachers) in all schools throughout the district. The survey was administered twice: just a few months prior to the appointment of a new superintendent and again four years later. We conducted interviews with board trustees at the end of year two of our district study.

Our interviews and engagement with school board trustees revealed that the collaborative processes that were promoted throughout the district were emerging among school board trustees as well (Brown, Dibbon, & Sheppard, 2003). In fact, the school board trustees invited us to share our understandings of the concept of collaborative leadership and organizational learning with them during two two-day retreats that occurred consecutively at the end of year one and year three of our partnership. During interviews one trustee credited the district office staff with having the foresight to create a collaborative environment for trustees. He observed that this collaboration occurred informally before and after school board and committee meetings and formally at committee and board meetings and at such events as retreats and conferences (personal communication, April 2003). Another trustee was impressed that the superintendent had sought school board permission to have his assistant superintendents attend board meetings. She had served on other boards where no other senior staff member but the CEO could attend board meetings. She felt that having other senior staff at board meetings contributed to a more open discussion that led to a more trusting relationship between the board and the senior administrative staff. Moreover, she felt that there was a general feeling of openness in the board and noted that her fellow trustees were interested in learning and that learning was greatly enhanced through the increased use of study sessions in which "open and frank" discussions were encouraged (personal communications, March 2003).

Analysis of our survey data of teachers' perceptions supports our qualitative findings that there was a shift toward a more collaborative approach to leadership and decision-making over the four-year period of our study. A comparison of teachers' perceptions of leadership approach prior to the superintendent's articulation of a vision of collaborative leadership and four years later revealed a statistically significant shift in perceptions that leadership in schools and throughout the district had become more collaborative (Welch[2] Statistic $(1, 289.96) = 212.1$, $p < .001$), a large effect size ($d = 1.6$) (Cohen, 1988).

Aside from teachers' perceptions of leadership approach, we were interested in determining the level to which they felt engaged in collaborative activities in their schools. Our analysis revealed a statistically significant positive shift in their perceptions of levels of collaboration from year one to year four (ANOVA,

---

[2] We employed the Welch statistic rather than the standard F statistic in order to account for heterogeneity.

$F(1, 440) = 37.17$, $p < .001$) as well. The magnitude of this effect is moderate ($d = 0.64$). Specific examples of this shift include a 33% increase in the level to which they perceived that structures were in place to support collaboration, a 16% increase in the level to which decision-making was perceived to be shared at the school level, and an 8% perceived increase in the level of their involvement in decision-making at the district level.

We also assessed teachers' perception of their level of engagement in dialoguing. Having argued that engagement in dialogue is essential to meaningful collaboration, we posited that if we found a statistically significant increase in the extent to which teachers perceived that they were engaged in dialogue in their schools, it would be further confirmation that the level of teacher involvement in collaboration had increased. Our results revealed a statistically significant increase in their perceptions of their level of engagement in dialogue from year one to year four (ANOVA, $F(1, 346) = 26.75$, $p < .001$) with a moderate effect size ($d = 0.56$).

Using multiple regression analysis, we determined that leadership that was perceived to be collaborative, inclusive, goal oriented, democratic, and supportive accounted for 38.3% of the variance in teachers' engagement in collaborative activities within their school ($R^2 = 0.383$, $F(5, 279) = 34.7$, $p < .001$), a large effect. When combined with the images accumulated through our qualitative data analysis of district-level processes, the evidence suggests that the superintendent's sharing of his vision of leadership and the creation of structures such as GAC, the Families of Schools, and the shared decision-making matrices contributed to significant growth in the level of engagement of constituents in school and district leadership.

Conclusion

While traditional school districts with their hierarchical and bureaucratic structures have been shown to inhibit the development of schools as professional learning communities, school districts can facilitate meaningful school reform through the creation of collaborative structures and mechanisms for meaningful shared decision-making. However, because most school districts and schools continue to cling to traditional bureaucratic structures, shifting to an empirically based leadership approach that is more collaborative and inclusive requires more than an expression of intent. The documented failure of many well-intentioned reform efforts with such labels as site-based management, shared decision-making, or teacher empowerment is good evidence that adopting the concepts alone will not suffice. We are convinced that deliberate leadership efforts such as those described in this chapter that are directed at replacing inhibiting traditional structures with those that are facilitative of a collaborative leadership approach, collaborative processes, and shared decision-making are required. Perhaps of most significance is that we have revealed clearly that while the implementation of collaborative structures that are facilitative of a collaborative approach to leadership and organizational learning throughout a school district is complex and full of risks, it can be achieved if deliberately championed by a leader committed to engaging others in the process.

References

Argyris, C. (1982). *Reasoning, learning and action: Individual and organizational.* New York: Basic Books.
Argyris, C. (1999). *On organizational learning.* Malden, MA: Blackwell.
Bass, B., & Riggio, R. (2006). *Transformational leadership.* Mahwah, NJ: Lawrence Erlbaum.
Barth, R. (1990). *Improving schools from within.* San Francisco, CA: Jossey-Bass.
Barth, R. (2001). *Learning by heart.* San Francisco, CA: Jossey-Bass.
Berends, M., Bodilly, S., & Kirby, S. (2002). Looking back over a decade of whole school reform: The experience of New American Schools. *Phi Delta Kappan, 84*(2), 168–175.
Bimber, B. (1994). *The decentralizing mirage: Comparing decision-making arrangements in four high schools* (MR-459-GGF-LE). Santa Monica, CA: RAND. Retrieved January 28, 2006 from http://www.rand.org/pubs/online/education/index.html.
Bodilly, S., Keltner, B., Purnell, S., Reichardt, R., & Schuyler, G. (1998). *Lessons from New American Schools' scale-up phase: Prospects for bringing designs to multiple schools.* Santa Monica, CA: Rand. Retrieved January 28, 2006 from http://www.rand.org/pubs/online/education/index.html.
Brown, J., Dibbon, D., & Sheppard, B. (2003, May). *The school trustee in a learning environment.* Annual Conference of CSSE, Halifax, Nova Scotia, Canada.
Bryk, A. S., & Schneider, B. (2003). Trust in schools: A core resource for school reform. *Educational Leadership, 60*(6), 40–44.
Clem, J., & Battino, W. (2006). A systemic change experience in the Chugach School District. *TechTrends, 50*(2), 35.
Cohen, J. (1988). *Statistical power analysis for the behavioural sciences.* New Jersey, NY: Lawrence Erlbaum.
Datnow, A. (2005). The sustainability of comprehensive school reform models in changing district and state contexts. *Educational Administration Quarterly, 41*(1), 121–153.
Doyle, M., & Straus, M. (1982). *How to make meetings work.* New York: Berkley Publishing.
Duffy, F. (2003). I think therefore I am resistant to change. *National Staff Development Council, 24*(1), 30–36.
Dufour, R., & Eaker, R. (1998). *Professional learning communities at work: Best practices for enhancing student achievement.* Alexandria, CA: Association for Supervision and Curriculum Development.
Dunlap, D., & Goldman, P. (1991, February). Rethinking power in schools. *Educational Administration Quarterly, 27* (1), 5–29.
Firestone, W., Mangin, M., Martinez, C., & Polovsky, T. (2005). Leading coherent professional development: A comparison of three districts. *Educational Administration Quarterly, 41*(3), 413–448.
Freire, P. (2004). Pedagogy of the oppressed. In D. J. Flinders & S. J. Thornton (Eds.), *The curriculum studies reader* (pp. 125–133). New York: Routledge Falmer.
Fullan, M. (1993). *Change forces.* London: Falmer Press.
Fullan, M. (1995). The school as a learning organization: Distant dreams. *Theory into Practice, 34*(4), 230–235.
Fullan, M. (2001). *Leading in a culture of change.* San Francisco, CA: Jossey-Bass.
Fullan, M. (2005). *Leadership and sustainability.* Thousand Oaks, CA: Corwin.
Galbraith, J., & Lawler, E. (1993). *Organizing for the future.* San Francisco, CA: Jossey Bass.
Gardner, J. (1990). *On leadership.* New York, NY: Free Press.
Green, R., & Etheridge, C. (2001). Collaboration to establish standards and accountability: Lessons learned about systemic change. *Education, 121*(4), 821.
Hall, G., & Hord, S. (2006). *Implementing change: Patterns, principles, and potholes.* Toronto: Pearson Education.
Hansen, J., & Roza, M. (2005). *Decentralized decision making for schools: New promise for an old idea.* Santa Monica, CA: Rand. Retrieved January 28, 2006 from http://www.rand.org/pubs/online/education/index.html

References

Hargreaves, A., & Evans, R. (1997). Teachers and educational reform. In A. Hargreaves & R. Evans (Eds.), *Beyond educational reform: Bringing teachers back in (pp. 1–18)*. Philadelphia: Open University Press

Harris, A. (2005). Leading or misleading? Distributed leadership and school improvement. *Journal of Curriculum Studies, 37*(3), 255–265.

Honig, M. (2003). Building policy from practice: District central office administrators' roles and capacity for implementing collaborative education policy. *Educational Administration Quarterly. 39*(3), 292–338.

Kouzes, J., & Posner, B. (2003). *Credibility*. San Francisco, CA: Jossey-Bass.

Lambert, L. (2005). What does leadership capacity really mean? *Journal of Staff Development. 26*(2), 39–40.

Leavitt, H. (2003). Why hierarchies thrive. *Harvard Business Review*, March, 96–102.

Leithwood, K., Leonard, L., & Sharratt, L. (2000). Conditions fostering organizational learning in schools. In K. Leithwood (Ed.), *Understanding schools as intelligent systems* (pp. 99–124). Stamford CT: JAI Press.

Leithwood, K., Louis, K., Anderson, S., & Wahlstrom, K. (2004). *How leadership influences student learning*. Retrieved Nov. 28, 2005 from http://www.wallacefoundation.org/WF/KnowledgeCenter/KnowledgeTopics/EducationLeadership/HowLeadershipInfluencesStudent Learning.htm

Mintzberg, H. (1973). *The nature of managerial work*. New York: Harper and Row.

Murphy, J. (2007, June). *Teacher leadership: Barriers and supports*. Paper presented at Teacher Working Conditions that Matter: The Symposium. Toronto, ON, Canada.

O'Toole, J. (1996). *Leading change*. Toronto: Jossey-Bass.

Peterson, K. (1982). Making sense of principals' work. *The Australian Administrator, 2*, 1–4.

Peterson, K., & Cosner, S. (2005). Teaching your principal. *Journal of Staff Development, 26*(2), 28–32.

Rusch, E. (2005). Institutional barriers to organizational learning in school systems: The power of silence. *Educational Administration Quarterly, 41*(1), 83–120.

Schein, E. (1993). On dialogue, culture, and organizational learning. *Organizational Dynamics, 22*(2), 40–51.

Schlechty, P. (1990). *Schools for the 21st century*. San Francisco, CA: Jossey-Bass.

Schlechty, P. (1997). *Inventing better schools: An action plan for education reform*. San Fransico, CA: Jossey-Bass.

Senge, P. (1990). *The fifth discipline*. New York: Doubleday.

Senge, P., Roberts, C., Ross, R., Smith, B., & Kleiner, A. (1994). *The fifth discipline fieldbook*. Toronto: Doubleday.

Sheppard, B., & Brown, J. (2006, October). *A CEO's five year journey: Translating theory into practice*. Paper presented at Commonwealth Council for Educational Administration and Management, Nicosia, Cyprus.

Sheppard, B., & Brown, J. (2007, April). *The CEO as an emergent leader in a school district hierarchy: Challenges and opportunities*. Paper presented at American Educational Research Association, Chicago.

Sheppard, B. (1996). Exploring the transformational nature of instructional leadership. *Alberta Journal of Educational Research, 42*(4), 325–344.

Sheppard, B. (2003). If to do in schools were as easy as to know what were good to do. *Education Canada, 43*(4), 16–19.

Silins, H., & Mulford, B. (2002). Schools as learning organisations: The case for system, teacher and student learning. *Journal of Educational Administration, 40*(5), 425–446.

Sparks, D. (2005). The final 2%. *Journal of Staff Development, 26*(2), 2–15.

Swinnerton, J. (2007). Brokers and boundary crossers in an urban school district: Understanding central-office coaches as instructional leaders. *Journal of School Leadership, 17*(2), 195–221.

Tschannen-Moran, M., & Hoy, W. K. (2000). A multidisciplinary analysis of the nature, meaning, and measurement of trust. *Review of Educational Research, 70*(4), 547–593.

Wenger, E. (1998). *Communities of practice: Learning, meaning, and identity*. Cambridge, England: Cambridge University Press.

Wynn, R., & Guiditus, C. (1984). *Team management: Leadership by consensus*. Toronto: Charles E. Merrill.

York-Barr, J., & Duke, K. (2004). What do we know about teacher leadership? Findings from two decades of scholarship. *Review of Educational Research, 74*(3), 255–316.

Chapter 5
Strategic Thinking and Adaptive Learning

Abstract There is little doubt that schools no longer function as closed systems as was largely the case until the latter part of the twentieth century and that they have become a part of a large complex adaptive system. Having accepted that reality, we recognize that the traditional approach to strategic planning—consulting selected stakeholders (assessment), writing a plan (planning), announcing implementation of the plan (implementation), and evaluating the planned outcomes (evaluation)—will likely result in disappointment. More contemporary models facilitate members engaging in formal planning, not to create strategies, but to program the strategies they already have, that is, to elaborate and operationalize their consequences formally. Examples of these more contemporary models of strategic planning are rare; however, this chapter will document one such experience. We trace one superintendent's journey as he works through strategic thinking and adaptive learning to establish a collaborative culture and a shared vision of professional learning in a school district steeped in bureaucratic thinking, while operating in an era of government accountability and mandated change. In the end, we acknowledge that the bureaucratic contexts in which school boards and provinces or states govern education often make it very difficult to plan strategically within an organizational learning framework. This case exemplifies this principle.

The existing strategic planning model imposed upon public bodies such as schools and school boards in many provinces throughout Canada (e.g., British Columbia, 2008; CCAF-FCVI, 2008; Newfoundland & Labrador, 2000, 2002, 2005; Nova Scotia, 2007; Saskatchewan, 2006) appears to be designed with the "good intention" of supporting systemic, sustainable reform (Sackney, 2007). In practice, however, it tends to inhibit meaningful educational change as most models continue to rely upon a traditional approach to planning that has been recognized as passé (Hamel, 2001; Mintzberg, 1994; Mintzberg & Lampel, 2001; Pascale, 2001; Reeves, 2002; Redding & Catalanello, 1992). Indeed, similar to strategic planning practices in other agencies, conventional government planning practices appear to have "changed hardly at all during the past decade or two" (Hamel, 2001, pp. 186–187), and rather than producing strategy, they produce plans.

Strategic planning has its roots in the military, so it is not surprising that in its earliest models, strategic planning embraced a top-down leadership approach where leaders at the top of the organization analyzed various situations and decided the direction of the organization (Lane, Bishop, & Wilson-Jones, 2005). Mintzberg (1994) contends that conventional planning models fit best in the machine organization (classic bureaucracy) that is epitomized by formalization, centralized authority, and standardization of work and stability. In such hierarchical, highly bureaucratic environments, planning is predicated on the lack of organizational capacity and the powerlessness of others to bring about meaningful change. As a consequence, initiatives are centrally mandated through a strategic plan that acts as blinders to horses to keep them going in the desired direction. This approach may work well in rather stable environments, but is problematic in dynamic environments like schools and school districts that are loosely coupled, operate according to deeply held cultural norms, and have to worry about constant change, shifting public priorities, and unforeseen competition. Mintzberg (1994) concludes that in these environments, the imposition of the conventional strategic planning models results in a huge waste of time and resources. In his view, these models assume

> that strategies should emanate from the top of the organization full-blown, that goals can be clearly stated, that the central formulation of strategies must be followed by their pervasive implementation, that the workers (in this case ... teachers, ... etc.) will (or must) respond to these centrally imposed strategies, and so on .... These assumptions are wrong, stemming from a misunderstanding of (or unwillingness to understand) how nonmachine forms of organization must function. The result has been a great deal of waste, trying to fit the square pegs of planning into round holes of organization. (pp. 404–405)

Similarly, McHenry and Achilles (2002) suggest that the strategic planning format employed by business has met with generally low levels of success within the education community because it attempts to modify existing business models to the unique demands of education planning (p. 2). Correspondingly, the Strategic Planning Roundtable (1993) cautions that "goals established through strategic planning may ... hamper ... the flexibility [that] schools of the future will need to be responsive to changing educational demands" (p. 4). Believing in the accuracy of this perspective, we concur with a growing number of others that the greatest difficulty with traditional models of strategic planning is the linear approach to planning, which is unable to account for changes in the environment.

Schools of today have become just one component of a complex adaptive organizational system that is composed of multiple dynamic interrelated subsystems consisting of other schools, the local community, the school district, and other levels of the environment that mutually determine one another's and the organization's directions (Pascale, 2001). In such an environment,

> strategy ... is always in development, always changing, always moving further into the future, based on a sense of the past and a sense of the dynamics in the world and the possibilities offered by the external and internal environment. (Goho & Webb, 2003, pp. 378–379)

Additionally, cause and effect cannot be easily identified. As a consequence, school members must focus on strategic thinking and adaptive learning rather than on traditional school development or strategic planning models (Emery, 2006; Pascale, 2001). Such an approach recognizes that change is complex and adaptive and that it occurs through a multiple dynamic interrelated web of learning cycles of successes and failures that simultaneously, consecutively, and intermittently spiral forward in a nonlinear fashion (Sheppard & Brown, 2000) (see Fig. 5.1). It recognizes that educational professionals in schools and school districts are always in the midst of complex change processes and that they must understand these processes in order to manage the complexities in ways that are productive for their schools and students.

There is little doubt that schools no longer function as closed systems as was largely the case until the latter part of the twentieth century and that they have become a part of a large complex adaptive system. Having accepted that reality, we recognize that the traditional approach to strategic planning—consulting selected stakeholders (assessment), writing a plan (planning), announcing implementation of the plan (implementation), and evaluating the planned outcomes (evaluation)—will likely result in disappointment. While this approach is often depicted as cyclical similar to Fig. 5.2, it is rarely more than a strictly linear process that is more accurately displayed in Fig. 5.3. Alternatively, within a strategic thinking and adaptive learning framework, members "engage in formal planning, not to create strategies but to program the strategies they already have, that is to elaborate and operationalize their consequences formally" (Mintzberg, 1994, p. 336) or as Fullan (1993) notes in his *Change Forces* "vision emerges ... from action" (p. 28). This, however, does not imply that schools or school districts should not engage in consultation with their school community or that they should not develop strategic visions. Actually, the development of a shared vision is a vital component of strategic thinking. While that vision may get somewhat adjusted during the change journey (as it emerges

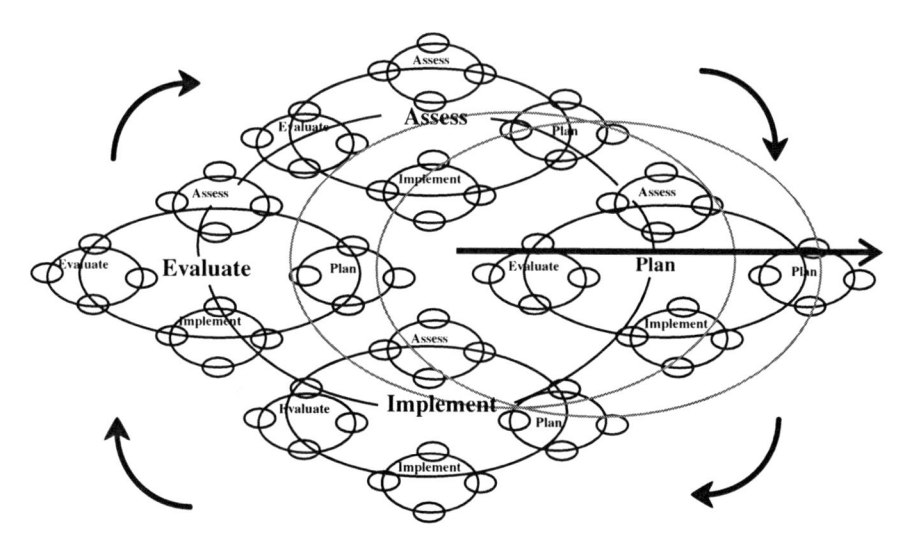

Fig. 5.1 Strategic thinking and adaptive learning cycle

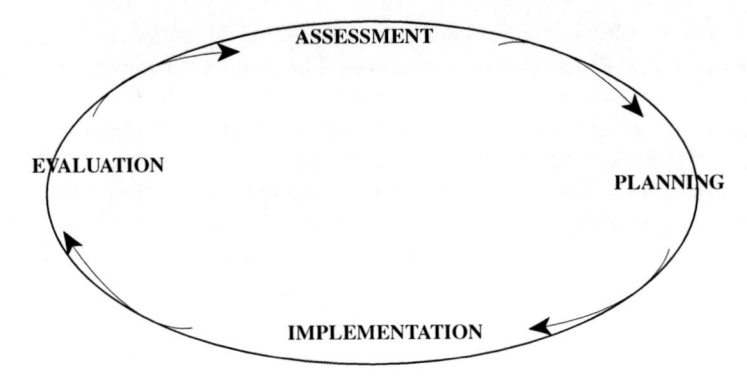

Fig. 5.2 Traditional strategic planning cycle

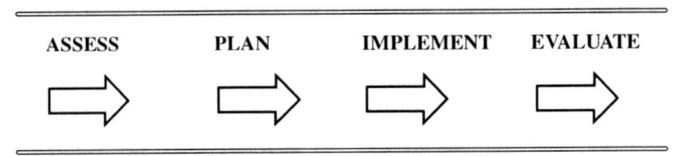

Fig. 5.3 Linear strategic planning approach

and reemerges from action), and it is anticipated that there will be many detours on the way, the shared vision provides the general compass bearing throughout the journey (Senge, Roberts, Ross, Smith, & Kleiner, 1994). Moreover, we share the view with some others that in education, shared vision is essential to maintaining a moral purpose that is focused on improving learning for each student (Dufour, 2004; Fullan, 1993, 1999; Hall & Hord, 2006).

Unfortunately, examples of successful implementation of these more contemporary models are almost as elusive as the proverbial "fountain of youth." Fortunately, this chapter will document one such experience as we trace one superintendent's journey as he works to establish a culture of collaboration and to create a shared vision of professional learning through strategic thinking and adaptive learning in a school district steeped in bureaucratic thinking while operating in an era of government accountability and mandated change.

My Voice

Strategic Planning in Discovery School District

As noted previously, most school districts and schools continue to operate as traditional hierarchical bureaucracies where the common expectation is that someone at the top of the organization will set the direction. Discovery School District was no different, and I knew that I had some significant challenges ahead of me. The traditional bureaucratic, hierarchical structure was deeply ensconced in the mindscapes of school board trustees, school district and school personnel, and the general public, and just a few months prior to my assuming the role as superintendent, the school board had completed the development of a strategic plan. As noted in previous chapters, I believed that the path that would most likely lead to district improvement was to shift the district away from a traditional bureaucratic hierarchy toward a professional learning community. This would require shifting toward collaborative leadership and eliminating existing structural barriers that might impede that shift. It was unlikely that engaging the school board and various constituents in another strategic planning process would assist in my achieving that goal.

The school board's strategic plan had been developed by the senior district administrators and a steering committee through consultations with district schools and communities, and it had been approved by the school board and distributed to all schools. It contained an articulated mission statement as follows: "Discovery School District, in partnership with the home and community, is committed to providing a supportive and dynamic learning environment dedicated to excellence in the total development of all learners" (*Discovery School District Strategic Plan*, 2000, p. 6). Central to the plan was a list of 10 goals of which "a focus on student learning" was just one. None of the goals were given any particular priority, nor were they accompanied by implementation plans, strategies, or guiding practices that would provide any shared images of the desired goal. There was no one assigned to champion either the further development of the plan or its implementation; there was no indication of how it would be resourced, and no accountability mechanisms were articulated. This plan as developed and written, for the most part, appeared to be consistent with those that have been found to yield little meaningful improvement (Reeves, 2002). It appeared to me that the 10 goals were simply representative of the major popular ideas, all of which were included in order to ensure collective buy-in. Of particular concern to me was the fact that several goals (e.g., to build a progressive and dynamic identity for the district) were likely to divert attention away from the focus on student learning, which I believed should be the primary mission of the school district.

A positive aspect of this plan, however, was its articulation of the inherent weaknesses of traditional strategic planning approaches and its embracing of a strategic thinking and adaptive learning approach to planning. It contained a clear statement that the written plan was "a living document designed to merge action and planning in a continuous cycle of action, reflection, and adjustment" (*Discovery School District Strategic Plan*, 2000, p. 14). This statement provided me with the flexibility needed to engage in strategic thinking and adaptive learning in the pursuit of educational reform that would bring about improved student learning throughout the district.

Because I took up my position as the superintendent of education toward the end of a school year, it was annual report time. In preparation for writing the board's annual report, I was required to review the annual reports submitted by school principals and other district educational personnel. As I began this process, I was struck by the lack of coherence between submissions and the articulated goals of board's strategic plan. None of the submissions addressed either the board's articulated mission or its goals. While I recognized that the board's strategic plan had just recently been released, it was surprising that there was no reference to it. After all, the plan had been in the making for at least two years, and I was aware that draft versions of this document had been available to district personnel and school principals for some time. Surely, I thought, they would not have to await the release of a formalized version of the strategic plan to know the primary goals of the district and to begin to pursue them. It appeared that up to this point in time, at least, the strategic plan was perceived to be little more than a document that had been developed to satisfy a government mandate and that few believed that it would guide future actions (Hamel, 2001; Reeves, 2002).

As the superintendent of education, I was acutely aware that the strategic plan was a school board document for which I was going to be held accountable, and as a result I assumed the role as its champion. My first attempt to highlight the importance of the strategic plan and its vision and goals was to require each district office contributor to the school board's annual report to rethink their contributions within the context of the strategic plan and to address each of the articulated goals. That activity was designed to provide an assessment of the relevance of the particular division's initiatives and activities in respect to the strategic goals and the articulated vision.

While there was some "pushback" from some individuals, I and my critical friends believed that this was a direction-changing moment as it created an authentic opportunity for district-level leaders to see the importance of having a clearly articulated shared vision that was connected to their work as well as to experience a first-hand glimpse of how all members of the organization could be held accountable for progress.

At the first GAC meeting at the commencement of the following school year, I drew attention to the need to connect the school development plans with the district strategic plan and to connect both to the school board's annual report. Moreover, I shared with the group my review of the emerging literature related to strategic planning and highlighted the importance of strategic thinking and adaptive learning. During group discussions, it became apparent that most were unaware that the existing district strategic planning document referenced that the plan would be implemented according to an organizational learning model and, in fact, the majority admitted that they had not viewed it as having any meaningful relevance for their school. At this meeting, GAC committed to working within the general vision and framework of the district strategic plan that the school board had approved, while giving particular priority to the core purpose of student learning. Throughout the course of that first semester, as GAC members gained confidence in collaborative processes (Chapter 4) and developed a more in-depth understanding of the complexity of the multiple factors that impacted student learning, we reached consensus that the district's primary strategic focus would be on improving classroom practices. This decision to focus on classroom practices led to the development of (1) a decision-making matrix on teaching and learning (see Chapter 4), (2) a new model of professional development (see Chapter 6), and (3) the development of a shared vision of teaching and learning (see Fig. 5.4) that would guide strategic thinking and action related to improvements in classroom practice. A discussion of the process of developing that shared vision follows.

Discovery School District Our Vision for Teaching and Learning

Our Statement of Vision

The purpose of teaching in Discovery School District is to challenge and develop the learning and achievement capabilities of each student in a safe, caring, and socially-just learning environment. Because teaching and learning is a complex dynamic process, teachers constantly strive to gain more knowledge and understanding of the research about how the human brain learns in order to improve their teaching methods. Our best practices are based on research, and our vision for teaching and learning evolves accordingly.

As a starting point, teaching and learning in Discovery School District occur as concurrent processes that accommodate each child's prior knowledge and varied learning style; emphasize movement and healthy living; and provide predictability and safety, social support, collaboration between adults and peers, sense of control, time on task, relevant content, and prompt feedback.

Images of Our Vision in Practice (What does it look like?)

Teachers commit to making a difference in the life of each student.

- Teachers take responsibility for each child's learning and achievement.
- Teachers ensure that no child is caught in an experience of low expectations.
- Teachers design learning opportunities that focus on providing learning opportunities that focus on the learning needs of each student.
- Teachers show sensitivity and attentiveness to the learner's previous knowledge and personal interests.
- Students know that teachers are concerned about them as individuals.

Teachers are accountable for the accomplishment of the learning outcomes set for each student.

- Teachers talk with students about their future ambitions and help them explore other options.
- Teachers help students explore opportunities by making connections between curriculum content and career opportunities.
- Teachers are familiar with the curriculum outcomes of all the courses/programs that they teach and design instruction and assessment on the basis of these outcomes and student needs.
- When individual students have unique needs that will require modification of standard provincial curriculum outcomes, teachers lead a team to appropriately modify the outcomes to meet those needs.
- Teachers ensure that the learning of curriculum outcomes is sequenced and that instructional time frames are set at the beginning of the school year.
- Teachers communicate the expected learning outcomes to students and parents.

Fig. 5.4 (continued)

- Teachers employ a variety of instructional strategies that account for differing learning styles and individual student needs.
- Teachers use assessment and evaluation strategies to regularly measure student mastery and achievement of specified learning outcomes, as an accountability measure and feedback mechanism for both learners and teachers.
- Teachers reflect on internal and external test results to assess the level of success of teaching-learning practices and to make any appropriate adjustments.
- Teachers use assessment results to modify learning opportunities to ensure the success of each student.
- Teachers assess learning related to expected learning outcomes and assign grades based on achievement of these outcomes over time, rather than on cumulative averages of discrete assessments.
- Teachers ask students to keep track of their own performance on the learning goals.
- To meet the learning needs of each student, teachers employ a variety of evaluation strategies that include the following: student conferencing, observations, oral presentations, group work, projects and assignments, unit tests, and major examinations.
- Co-curricular programs are designed to complement and support the core curriculum to ensure a focus on all of the Provincial Essential Graduation Learnings: Aesthetic Expression, Citizenship, Communication, Personal Development, Problem Solving, Spiritual and Moral Development, and Technological Competence.

Teaching engages learners in dynamic, interactive, motivating, meaningful, hands-on, integrated, and creative learning experiences that include direct instruction, experiential learning, group work, individualized instruction, home study, and digital learning.

- Instruction varies depending upon the need, but no teacher depends exclusively upon one instructional approach.
- A student in any single class experiences minimally each of the following as a matter of routine:
  - experimentation
  - authentic experiences (e.g., field trips)
  - simulations (e.g., computer simulations, role play).
  - visiting resource people
  - cooperative learning (structured group work)
  - homework and home study
  - problem-solving sessions
  - teacher-centered oral question and answer sessions
  - teacher presentation
  - independent work
  - project-based learning
  - resource-based and computer technology-assisted learning

Teaching takes place in a caring, co-operative, nurturing, inclusive, structured, resource-rich environment with routines of high expectations, and mutual respect. There is an emphasis on the development of self-discipline and responsibility; however, appropriate consequences for violation of school and classroom rules and procedures are well established.

Fig. 5.4 (continued)

- Displays in each classroom are related to current learning objectives, are appropriate to student interests, and are designed to motivate learning.
- Displays in each classroom celebrate student learning.
- Teachers serve as role models for attendance, promptness, and efficiency.
- Teachers and students hold high expectations for one another.
- Classroom routines are well established and students and teachers are conscious of efficient use of time in all classroom activities.
- Teachers and students collaboratively create a learning environment conducive to learning in a climate of respect and responsibility.
- Teachers praise students for achievement and challenge negative attitudes and behaviors.
- All students know what is expected of them.
- Teachers establish an ethos where each student feels safe and valued.

Parents and other community members are considered partners in support of student learning.

- School councils are focused on the continued improvement of teaching and learning.
- Processes are in place to involve parent and community directly and indirectly in facilitating student learning.
- Teachers communicate the expected student learning outcomes to parents.
- Teachers use multiple types of assessment data when communicating student learning success to parents.
- Training and support are provided to parents to enhance their parenting skills and to improve communication with their children so they can better support their children's learning.

Teachers are reflective professionals who engage in collaborative leadership to continuously improve the norms and practices of their profession and the teaching and learning environment of the entire school.

- Teachers view themselves and their colleagues as innovators.
- Teachers are informed professionals who are aware of the emerging research literature on multiple intelligences and brain-compatible learning and are anxious to alter practices based on this emerging research.
- Teachers are anxious to explore and engage in reflective practice of new instructional strategies that hold promise for improved student learning.
- Teachers collaboratively develop school growth plans that are focused on improved teaching and learning practices and hold one another accountable for the implementation of that plan.
- Teachers are leaders in the change process.
- Teachers engage in personal and professional development that is based on individual needs in the context of goals, policies, and mandates of the school, district, and province.
- Teachers work collaboratively with other professionals to develop units of work and to improve practice.
- Teachers share in school-level decision-making related to teaching and learning according to defined protocols.

Fig. 5.4 Shared vision for teaching and learning

Developing a Shared Vision for Teaching and Learning

Having made the decision that we (GAC) would focus our attention on improving classroom practices, it was essential to establish a shared vision of practices toward which we would strive. We were quite conscious, however, that many teachers within the district were very skeptical of spending their valued time on the development of yet another "bland *motherhood and apple pie*" (Senge et al., 1994, p. 23) vision that they had come to recognize as having no relevance to their practice. This was made quite evident to us through a survey that we (the critical friends' research team) had conducted just one year earlier. Results had revealed that only 36% of the teachers surveyed considered vision statements to be useful in guiding practice. Being aware of this, GAC set out to co-create a shared vision for teaching and learning that included images of the future that the engaged constituents (teachers, program specialists, principals, and other senior district office educational professionals) wished to create, together with the principles, guiding practices, and processes that would help them achieve these collective images (Senge et al.).

As a consequence of my previous work with the district as a critical research friend, I was aware that the project team for a learning school/classroom practices research project had developed an outline of exemplary teaching and learning classroom practices (see Chapter 6 for more information about this project). I reminded other members of the Administrative Council of this outline, and we agreed that it would serve as an excellent starting point for the co-creation of a shared vision for teaching and learning. Those of us who shared the view that this outline represented a good starting point for a vision that we could personally support as our personal professional vision accepted the responsibility for sharing it throughout the district. We agreed to emphasize during each presentation that we were not presenting this vision as something that we expected others to endorse. Our objective was to share our vision in order to encourage individuals to engage in personal refection as a point of departure for the development of a vision for teaching and learning that would be shared by all teacher professionals throughout the district.

I shared my vision at GAC, at various schools where I was invited to speak, and at two major district-wide conferences that together included all professional educators in the school district. During each of these conferences, morning parallel sessions were devoted to preliminary dialogue about the vision statements that I had shared, about their individual personal vision for teaching and learning, and about the goal of developing a shared vision for the school district. Following the conferences, school principals led the co-creation of a shared vision in their individual schools and acted as boundary spanners between the teachers in their individual schools and GAC. This process of co-creation continued for approximately two years. The final Discovery School District vision for teaching and learning included a listing of key principles, each of which were fully developed with descriptive images of preferred practices (see Fig. 5.4). These images were developed further through the creation of two videos (*Allow Me to Grow, k-6*, 2002; *Inside Out, 7–12*, 2003) that revealed the vision in practice in various classrooms throughout the district. These videos were made available to each school community; they were used in professional development sessions for teachers, and they showcased for the school board and parents what the teaching professionals of Discovery School District hoped teaching and learning would look like in classrooms throughout the district. This vision—and in particular the videos—generated a great deal of positive energy throughout the entire district. It was followed by the development of an implementation framework that would allow each teacher, each school, and the district to develop their unique plans for moving toward the shared vision. These plans served as the primary backdrop for all professional development in the district (see Fig. 5.5). This implementation framework and accompanying professional development support were endorsed by the school board as a component of the board's strategic plan—an example of "vision emerging from action."

Charting the Course

(How and when will we realize our vision?)

We will conduct assessments of the extent that our vision exists currently.

- Individual teachers will conduct a self assessment of the extent to which our Vision of Teaching and Learning exists within their classrooms.
- Each school will conduct an assessment of the extent to which our Vision of Teaching and Learning exists within the school.
- The District will conduct an assessment of the extent to which our Vision of Teaching and Learning exists in all schools throughout the district.

The following questions will guide each of the assessments:

- To what extent do(es) I/my school/all schools engage in the teaching and learning behaviours, norms, or practices that form the images of our vision?
- How much will a change in my/my school's/all schools' current practices toward the vision increase individual student learning and achievement?
- How much effort will it take to significantly change my/my school's/all schools' current practices so that our vision becomes a reality in my classroom/my school/all schools?
- What is a reasonable time frame for me/my school/all schools to significantly change current practices so that our vision becomes a reality.

We will employ the applicable growth plan to develop and implement a plan of action.

- Personal and Professional Growth Plans (individual teachers)
- School Growth Plans (schools)
- District Strategic Plan (all schools)

We will assess the level of success toward our vision for teaching and learning and its impact upon student learning and achievement at the individual, school, and district level according to a defined time line.

Fig. 5.5 Implementation framework

Personal Reflections

Even though the development of a shared vision for teaching and learning proved to be a very worthwhile process, I struggled from the beginning with my direct engagement in it. For me it presented two paradoxes. First, I was advocating collaborative leadership, and I was aware that an assistant superintendent had contributed to the initial development of the outline of the exemplary teaching and learning practices. I pondered, "Should I leave this file with him?" But on the other hand, I mused, "Given the culture of hierarchy and the typical lack of engagement of superintendents in matters directly related to teaching and learning, the level of my engagement might send a message about its relative importance within the district."

The second paradox was similar to that which I experienced in my initial sharing of my vision of leadership for the district (see Chapter 4). At that time, I sought direction from the relevant leadership literature, the school district administrative team, and my critical friends and decided to articulate my vision of leadership throughout the district. But teaching and learning was a different matter! Teachers themselves had considerable ownership of this area. Moreover, my communicating a personal vision had the potential of inhibiting the development of a vision that was genuinely co-created (Senge et al., 1994).

I shared my apprehensions at both an Administrative Council meeting and a GAC meeting, and at both there was a consensus that most teachers would likely expect the superintendent to have a personal vision of teaching and learning (Bass & Riggio, 2006; Kouzes & Posner, 2003). Furthermore, my articulating it would send a strong message that Discovery School District was placing a priority on teaching and learning. As for the issue of compromising the integrity of the co-creation process, we concluded that this should not be a concern as long as we provided teachers with a collegial hierarchy-free environment to develop their personal vision. Also, we concluded our vision could serve as a compass to be used by educators throughout the district while we were in the long process of co-creating a shared vision.

Whether my direct engagement in this process inhibited our efforts to break down the cultural barriers to collaborative leadership or whether it confounded the district's ability to create a vision that was truly shared may never be known. However, we do know that the process of creating a vision for teaching and learning in Discovery School District created a special synergy throughout the entire district that was motivating for educators, parents, and trustees and that it contributed to improved student learning.

A Final Observation

While I initially believed that the strategic plan that had been developed immediately prior to my assuming the role of superintendent was just another document that would serve little meaningful purpose, its design allowed for strategic thinking and adaptive learning. While the initial 10 goals of the strategic plan were unwieldy and typical of traditional strategic plans that have been much maligned, we were able to work with the school board and its stakeholders to reshape the strategic priorities to those that we deemed most important for the improvement of student learning. As a result we were able to develop a vision for education that was genuinely shared by teachers, administrators, and the other stakeholders in the district. Teachers and administrators accepted more responsibility for their own learning and began to dialogue more frequently about important educational issues; collaboration within and between schools became much more common; new programs were introduced and programs such as music, drama, the visual arts, French, and physical education were rejuvenated; and student academic performance began to improve as well.

By the fourth year, the strategic plan that I had inherited was fully redeveloped through a process of strategic thinking and adaptive learning that fully engaged district partners. The new redeveloped strategic plan comprised of only two goals: (1) to challenge and develop the learning and achievement capabilities of each student and (2) to create a safe, caring, and socially just learning environment. While it was formatted to meet perfunctory government requirements and approved by the school board with a supporting budget, the fundamental principle underlying it was organizational learning that required strategic thinking and adaptive learning.

When I left the district after my fourth year as superintendent, I could reflect on the experience and feel that I had left the district in a better position to learn than it was when I had inherited it. I had wanted the district to be a high-performance, professional learning community of enabled and empowered constituents who were engaged as leaders throughout the organization, and I think we had made a quantum leap toward that goal.

Through the Lens of Critical Friends

We have to admit that upon first reading the superintendent's *My Voice* claim that the original strategic plan (approved just prior to his appointment) provided direction for leadership actions throughout his four-year term as superintendent of education, we were skeptical. To us, it appeared that it served little more than to satisfy a legal mandate and to appease those school board trustees who felt some ownership of it. In response to our challenging him on his view, however, he insisted that it did remain as a foundational document until the development of a new strategic plan during the last year of his term as superintendent. In defense of his argument, he insisted that we once again review each of the school board's annual reports for that period. Our review revealed that each report provided a detailed account of the annual progress made on each of the 10 strategic goals of the original plan. He noted as well that the progress related to each of these goals continued to serve as a central component of his and his district staff's annual performance review (personal communication, August 2008). We suggest, though, that the accomplishment of the other goals such as "building a progressive and dynamic identity for Discovery School District" occurred only as a byproduct of the district's success related to its innovative teaching and improved student learning. And as we view it, in the final analysis, it was not the strategic plan that made the difference in this district. It was leadership, strategic thinking, and adaptive learning.

It is apparent that at the outset the superintendent struggled with what he perceived to be a conflict between his accountability to the school board to implement a strategic plan that in his view was seriously flawed and his commitment to organizational learning. It appears, however, that his understanding of strategic thinking and adaptive learning allowed him to navigate through this conflict and the challenges that he perceived to be inherent in the very document that was designed to support district growth. It is our view that without his in-depth understanding of strategic thinking and adaptive learning, it is highly likely that the plan would have been simply another document to gather dust on the shelf. While the authors of the strategic planning document made reference to organizational learning and noted that it was "intended to be a living document designed to merge action, reflection, and adjustment," evidence gathered from our involvement as critical research friends during that time suggests that the concept was poorly understood by key district leaders, with the exception of the program specialist who had written this portion of the document. In light of the fact that this specialist moved to a senior posting in another school district shortly after the plan was adopted, it was fortunate that the superintendent was aware of the empirical literature related to organizational learning, strategic thinking, and adaptive learning and knew how it applied to practice. We also believe that our engagement as critical friends throughout this period provided essential support as we provided opportunities for school board trustees to engage in research activities. We conducted a series of full-day seminars on organizational learning that engaged them in a variety of strategic thinking exercises designed to build their capacity for strategic thinking and adaptive learning.

Unfortunately, at the point that Discovery School District was poised to move forward with a new strategic plan, the district's life was cut short. At the end of the superintendent's fourth year, in a massive and sudden restructuring initiative, the ruling government arbitrarily consolidated 10 existing English-speaking school districts into four new districts. Discovery, which was really beginning to emerge as a provincial leader in many aspects of education, was consolidated with three existing boards to make one large school district, and its identity, along with its existing policies, structures, practices, and many existing relationships, was dissolved with the stroke of a pen in the provincial legislature. Just why the districts were consolidated has never been clearly articulated; however, the rhetoric of the time would lead us to believe it was an attempt by government to improve the operational efficiency of the administrative infrastructure and at the same time improve accountability measures by increasing the capacity of the districts to deliver educational services to students.

Over the last two decades much has been made of increasing levels of accountability in education both locally and globally. Many of these accountability measures have not met with the anticipated success (Fullan, 2005), and often the reason can be traced to incompatible agendas from governments, districts, and schools and to the absence of systemic thinking. That is an argument that can be made in this instance. We deal with this issue in more detail in Chapter 7, *Systems Challenges to Growth and Sustainability of Meaningful Educational Reform.*

In conclusion, we acknowledge that bureaucratic contexts in which school boards and provinces govern education often make it very difficult to plan strategically within an organizational learning framework, and this case exemplifies this principle. While the school board was very committed to working within that framework, government officials and the provincial school board's association often challenged their approach (superintendent's email archive). In respect to strategic planning and school development, government was following a very top-down, authoritarian approach that appeared to conform to that which Redding and Catalanello (1992) had eschewed nearly two decades ago as an ineffective first iteration of change where the plan was completed by senior administrators and/or a leadership team with an apparent assumption that because it was planned, it would be executed and change would occur. As researchers and students of change, we prefer to see a model similar to Redding and Catalanello's fourth iteration that emphasizes constant readiness, continuous planning, improvised implementation, and action learning, which is consistent with the strategic thinking and adaptive learning approach practiced in Discovery School District. Fortunately, Discovery School District was able to navigate successfully the divide between the government's mandated first iteration approach and the fourth iteration.

References

Bass, B., & Riggio, R. (2006). *Transformational leadership*. Mahwah, NJ: Lawrence Erlbaum.

British Columbia (2008). *District achievement contracts*. Retrieved May 10, 2008 from http://www.gov.bc.ca./bced/

CCAF~FCCAF (2008). *Public performance reporting*. Retrieved May 10, 2008 from http://www.performancereporting.ca/

Dufour, R. (2004). Leadership is an affair of the heart. *Journal of Staff Development, 25*(1), 67–68.

Emery, E. (2006). *The future of schools: How communities and staff can transform their school districts*. Toronto: Rowman and Littlefield Education.

Fullan, M. (1993). *Change forces*. London: Falmer Press.

Fullan, M. (1999). *Change forces: The sequel*. London: Falmer Press.

Fullan, M. (2005). *Leadership and sustainability*. Thousand Oaks, CA: Corwin.

Goho, J., & Webb, K. (2003). Planning for success: Integrating analysis with decision making. *Community College Journal of Research and Practice, 27*, 377–391.

Hall, G., & Hord S. (2006). *Implementing change: Patterns, principles, and potholes*. Toronto: Pearson Education.

Hamel, G. (2001). Strategy innovation and the quest for value. In M. Cusumano & C. Markides (Eds.), *Strategic thinking for the next economy* (pp. 181–195). San Francisco, CA: Jossey-Bass.

Kouzes, J., & Posner, B. (2003). *Credibility*. San Francisco, CA: Jossey-Bass.

Lane, R., Bishop, H., & Wilson-Jones, L. (2005). Creating an effective strategic plan for the school district. *Journal of Instructional Psychology, 32*(3), 197–204.

McHenry, W., & Achilles, C. (2002). *A district level planning model*. Paper presented at the annual meeting of the American Association of School Administrators, San Diego, California.

Mintzberg, H. (1994). *The rise and fall of strategic planning*. New York: Prentice-Hall.

Mintzberg, H. & Lampel, J. (2001). Reflecting on the strategic process. In M. Cusumano & C. Markides (Eds.), *Strategic thinking for the next economy* (pp. 9–32). San Francisco, CA: Jossey-Bass.

Newfoundland and Labrador. (2000). *Achieving excellence: A guidebook for the improved accountability of public bodies*. St. John's, NL: Government of Newfoundland and Labrador.

Newfoundland and Labrador (2002). *Excellence in strategic planning: A workshop for Newfoundland and Labrador School Board's Association*. St, John's NL: Author.

Newfoundland and Labrador. (2005). *Guidelines for multi-year performance-based planning*. St. John's, NL: Government of Newfoundland and Labrador. Retrieved March 2 from http://www.exec.gov.nl.ca/exec/cabinet/transacc/pdf/GuidelinesforPlanning.pdf

Nova Scotia. (2007). *Governing in the public sector*. Halifax, NS: Government of Nova Scotia, Retrieved March 2 from http://www.gov.ns.ca/tpb/

Pascale, R. (2001). Surfing the edge of chaos. In M. Cusumano & C. Markides (Eds.), *Strategic thinking for the next economy* (pp. 105–129). San Francisco, CA: Jossey-Bass.

Redding, J., & Catalanello, R. (1992, May). The fourth iteration: The learning organization as a model of strategic change. *Thresholds in Education*, 47–53.

Reeves, D. (2002). *The daily disciplines of leadership*. San Francisco, CA: Jossey-Bass.

Sackney, L. (2007). *Systemic reform for sustainability*. Government of Saskatchewan. Retrieved June 25, 2008 from http://www.publications.gov.sk.ca/

Saskatchewan. (2006). *Continuous improvement framework guide*. Retrieved June 25, 2008 from http://www.publications. gov.sk.ca/

Senge, P., Roberts, C., Ross, R., Smith, B., & Kleiner, A. (1994). *The fifth discipline fieldbook*. Toronto: Doubleday.

Sheppard, B., & Brown, J. (2000, April). *Pulling together or apart: Factors influencing a school's ability to learn*. Paper presented at the Annual Conference of the American Educational Research Association, New Orleans, US. http://www.eric.ed.gov/. ED443144.

Strategic Planning Roundtable. (1993). *Planning for change: A source book for strategic planning*. Durham, NH: New Hampshire Leadership Center.

Chapter 6
Professional Development and Capacity Building

Abstract Professional learning is critical to organizational effectiveness. Schools and school districts are composed of individuals, and these organizations learn and change only as individuals learn. Unfortunately, the traditional models of professional development have not really been successful in fostering individual professional learning or in changing individual's professional practices. This chapter describes the process of implementing a new model that shifts the focus from the traditional approach of professional development where either the "experts" or the formal leaders decide what is important for teachers to learn, to a focus on personal professional learning that assumes that organizations must support individuals as they strive to meet personal goals that are connected in meaningful ways with the organization. It assumes that the organization cannot force meaningful professional learning, but must establish conditions that encourage and support individuals to learn professionally. This chapter traces how this shift occurred and the challenges faced by the school district. It required not only changes in the culture, but also structural changes for district personnel to allow for personal choice.

The work of teaching professionals has become increasingly complex and demanding as schools and school districts have been increasingly held accountable for ensuring that nearly all students perform at high levels of academic achievement that was "once assumed to be the purview of a few" (Schlechty, 2001, p. 10). With this increased accountability, the expectation of the public and governments from schools and school districts is that they meet the diverse needs of individual learners so that each student will attain a high standard in the achievement of curriculum outcomes. In spite of such a lofty goal, little has been done to support teachers in its realization (Elmore, 2002; Liebeman, 1995; Smylie, 1996; Starratt, 2004). In essence, teachers are expected to accomplish this task as solo practitioners in their own classroom environments, and at the same time they are expected to contribute as teacher leaders in a school development process that theoretically should impact student learning (Glickman, Gordon, & Ross-Gordon, 2007; Ryan, 2006). This latter activity, school development, consumes a considerable portion of teachers' professional development time. For instance, Sheppard (2008) found that in one Canadian province, 86% of the teachers perceived school development planning to be the primary determiner of their professional development. Given that teachers often find that they do not have time to complete all the tasks related to their classroom responsibilities, they tend to resent the amount of time that they have to commit to school development planning as they perceive it to be related only remotely to their core classroom responsibilities (Ryan, 2006). On the other hand, professional development that is focused on classroom-related activities that might be viewed more positively by teachers occurs, predominantly, only when new curriculum is being introduced, and then it is rarely more than a one-shot event (Fullan, 2001; Sheppard, 2008). As a result, this too has "a terrible reputation among scholars, policymakers, and educators alike as being pedagogically unsound, economically inefficient, and of little value to teachers" (Smylie, 1996, p. 10). Having observed the limited attention given to professional development focused on the actual teaching and learning processes in the classroom, Elmore (2002) concluded that

> there are few portals through which new knowledge about teaching and learning can enter schools; few structures or processes in which teachers and administrators can assimilate, adapt, and polish new ideas and practices; and few sources of assistance for those who are struggling to understand the connection between academic performance of their students and the practices in which they engage. (p. 4–5)

It is apparent that rather than emphasizing professional development as a means of educational improvement, the most common approach is to hold teachers accountable without providing the necessary time and resources to build teachers' professional capacity. In our view, such an approach is based on a flawed theory of action "that the problems of schooling are due in large part to the lack of direction, excessive discretion, and low accountability within the education system" (Smylie, 1996, p. 9). If teachers are to be held accountable for meeting increasingly high expectations for the learning of all students, those holding the expectations must assume responsibility to provide teachers with the necessary professional development in order to develop their capacity to meet the demand. The imposition of bureaucratic work rules and procedures that often accompany the high expectations is simply wrongheaded (Elmore, 2002; Glickman et al., 2007). Sheppard (1996) found that meaningful professional development, on the other hand, not only contributes to the development of new classroom capabilities, but also leads to increased levels of teacher commitment to the school and their colleagues; it improves collegial collaboration and enhances teachers' willingness to experiment with new instructional approaches.

Our argument here, however, is not simply that teachers should be provided with opportunities for more professional development. As a matter of fact, in spite of considerable support for the importance of professional development to improved classroom practice, Sheppard (2008) found that 28% of the educational professionals in one Canadian province perceived their professional development experiences to be a waste of time and 38% viewed them as not relevant to their needs or the needs of their colleagues.

Having taken note of the weaknesses of the common approaches to professional development, Smylie (1996) recommends that if professional development is to lead to improved teaching practices,

> teachers' opportunities to learn should be problem oriented and grounded in inquiry, experimentation, and reflection. They should be collaborative, involving interaction with other teachers and education professionals as sources of new ideas and feedback. These opportunities should be coherent, intensive, and ongoing ... [and can occur through a variety of] structures and processes ... [that] include individually guided study, clinical supervision, and training; interactive learning from curriculum and instructional development and school improvement; and individual and collaborative inquiry, such as action and teacher research. (p. 10)

Results of a large-scale study of a professional development initiative in science and mathematics in the USA conducted by Garet, Porter, Desimone, Birman, and Yoon (2001) provide us with guidance for quality professional development as well. They found that reform-type professional development that includes mentoring, coaching, and study groups that often takes place during the regular school day was more effective than traditional activities such as workshops, institutes, courses, and conferences. Also, they found that professional development that engaged groups of teachers from the same school was longer in duration (both contact hours and time span), was focused on content knowledge, employed inquiry-oriented learning approaches, and was highly coherent with district directions and other professional development experiences was more likely to lead to an increase in teachers' knowledge and skills and to positively influence teaching practices.

Penuel, Fishman, Yamaguchi, and Gallagher (2007) found findings similar to those of Garet et al. (2001) with an important addition—the need to consider teachers, their context, their personal professional goals, and differing curricula:

> when considering how to "localize" their professional development activities, providers ... need to consider not only teachers' own contexts but also the program's demands on teachers and how those demands can be met within their contexts .... There must be a good "fit" between the curriculum and the local context, and ... fit is shaped partly by the effectiveness of the professional development activities themselves and also by the ability of providers to meet other demands of teachers and by teachers' own judgments about how coherent a program is with their personal professional goals and their goals for their students' learning. (p. 952)

Similarly, Borko (2004) concluded from her review of relevant empirical evidence that professional development experiences that explicitly focus on subject matter and how children's ideas about a subject develop can help teachers to better foster students' learning. Moreover, she concluded that the development of "strong professional communities can foster teacher learning" (p. 6) and instructional improvement.

Having reviewed the existing literature related to professional development, Glickman et al. (2007) concluded that a considerable knowledge base exists related to successful professional development programs and propose the following common characteristics that can serve as guidelines for improved practice:

1. Involvement of participants in planning, implementing, and evaluating programs
2. Programs that are based on schoolwide goals but that integrate individual and group goals with school goals
3. Long-range planning and development
4. Programs that incorporate research and best practice in school improvement and instructional improvement
5. Administrative support, including provision of time and other resources as well as involvement in program planning and delivery
6. Adherence to the principles of adult learning
7. Attention to the research on change, including the need to address individual concerns through the change process
8. Follow-up and support for transfer of learning to the school or classroom
9. Ongoing assessment and feedback
10. Continuous professional development that becomes part of the school culture. (pp. 353–354)

Hall and Hord (2006) view professional development as an essential component of educational reform, but emphasize the importance of placing an emphasis on individual teacher's learning rather than group learning. They contend that schools are composed of individuals and they (schools) learn only as teachers learn. Consequently, while many change processes can be directed at various groups, in the final analysis, it must be recognized that "successful change starts and ends at the individual level" (p. 7). Similarly, Senge, Roberts, Ross, Smith, and Kleiner (1994) highlight the importance of personal professional learning in their learning organization discipline of personal mastery. They contend that "the central tenet of this discipline [is that] no one can increase someone else's personal mastery. We can only set up conditions which encourage and support people who want to increase their own" (p. 193). A focus on personal professional learning shifts the model of learning away from traditional models, where either the "experts" or the "management personnel" decide what is important for employees to learn. The following conditions are necessary if personal professional learning is to be facilitated: (1) The organization must support individuals as they strive to meet personal goals that are connected in a meaningful way with the organization, (2) staff at all levels (including administration) must engage in relevant learning activities, (3) adequate support must be provided for individual engagement in learning, (4) all professional development and training opportunities must be relevant to the individual's learning need, and (5) there must be personal and organizational commitment to it.

It is this emerging knowledge base related to professional development that guided leadership practices of the superintendent of education and the work of the critical friends in Discovery School District.

Professional Development in Discovery School District

As the last five chapters have shown, Discovery School District's approach to leadership was based on a collaborative leadership and organizational learning framework.

This approach (more fully described in Chapter 2) requires that "knowledge have a shared, social construction common to all members of the school organization" (Louis, 2007, p. 4). It requires the facilitation of collaboration and distributed leadership roles as the school communities learn from each other (Senge et al., 1994). It requires a culture of trust and high expectations, where individuals feel valued and respected (Leithwood & Jantzi, 2005). This approach, in addition to the emerging literature related to professional development, had profound implications for professional development and capacity building within the school district even though it was tempered by the provincial context.

From a legal perspective, Discovery School District operated within a legislative framework and was dependent on government for its entire professional development budget including the allocation of professional development leave days (see Chapter 7 for a more detailed discussion of budgeting in Discovery School District). Government control of the professional development budget and the leave days limited the school district's discretion in respect to the amount of professional development available to individual teachers as there was little time available beyond that required for the mandated school development process and the implementation of new curriculum (Sheppard, 2008). The school district had little flexibility related to purpose and the amount available for professional development; in reality, however, it had considerable discretion over the nature of professional development, particularly in respect to school development.

Within that context, in the early years following its formation through government legislation in 1997, Discovery School District embarked on a number of initiatives. It was through the first school development initiative that we became involved as university critical friends aimed at developing teacher leadership and professional learning. Aside from the action learning/professional learning project, Discovery School District focused on implementing information communications technology (ICT) in all classrooms within the district and committed funds to ICT infrastructure development (high-speed connectivity with classroom access and network communication using Lotus Notes).

Professional development of teachers with limited time and resources revealed itself as a huge challenge. In order to finance their ICT initiatives, the district hired a partnership coordinator who developed school–community partnerships that enabled them to leverage external funds from external agencies (primarily through various federal government programs, which otherwise would not be accessible to schools or the school district). One such program provided ICT hardware and software to schools in order to provide community ICT access so that parents of the school and other community members could develop their own skills outside of regular school hours. The ICT infrastructure was available to teachers and students during the regular school day. Also, Discovery deployed technology resource teachers as a means of building capacity to support the implementation of ICT in classrooms. The improved capacity led to increased use of ICT in classrooms throughout schools in the district and contributed to the ability of schools to access additional federal funds through two other federal government initiatives: GrassRoots and the Network of Innovative Schools.

The ICT research and professional development initiatives in the Discovery schools had three components.

1. *The Learning School/Classroom.* The first component was based on the premise that if schools are to make meaningful improvements to support teaching and learning, they must increase their organizational capacity. Teams of teachers and researchers engaged in team learning and action research to implement ICT into teaching and learning at the classroom level. The target of our investigation as critical research friends was the relationship between leadership, organizational learning, and the implementation of innovative classroom practices with a particular focus on teaching and learning in the classroom. As part of this project, we worked with school district and department of education personnel to develop a list of teaching and learning practices that were considered within Discovery School District to be exemplary. For several years this appeared to have had little impact on teachers' professional development. Another project (the Xerox project) between the Faculty of Education, Discovery, and a private sector company allowed recent graduates with ICT skills to work in the classrooms as participant-observers where they provided technical support to classroom teachers, thereby providing a learning environment for teachers where they felt more comfortable in their initial use of the technology in their classroom practice.
2. *The Learning Community of Schools.* This component focused on the use of online professional development to support organizational learning and action research. The Internet provided the means that would allow teachers to move outside direct delivery mode into a virtual professional learning environment that was independent of unique school settings. Interschool collaboration allowed for opportunities for collaborative learning and organizational capacity building. Teachers from selected schools explored collaborative professional development using Learning Village software developed with IBM for the project (in partnership with the Faculty of Education, IBM and Discovery). In the development stage, we involved a different group of schools than the ones involved with the first component, the learning school/classroom. We anticipated that by engaging different schools, we would increase the level of collaboration throughout the district.
3. *The Learning School District.* The first two components were combined to build the organizational capacity of the school district and to explore the question, "Can ICT facilitate the creation of learning communities where there exists a culture of learning for all—a requirement if Canadians are to be leaders in the knowledge society?" It was hoped that each component would complement the other. The virtual professional development model (Learning Village) would allow interschool collaboration, through asynchronous access by individual teachers, that would facilitate across-school professional development activities that were grounded in successful practices emerging from the school-based component (team learning, action research, and organizational change). In principle, the combination would provide a model of collaboration, professional

development, and capacity building through the utilization of the capabilities of high-speed, multimedia networks that would also connect schools with parents and community.

In conjunction with the learning school district focus and as a result of the existing university–school district partnership, Discovery School District was invited to become a partner in a national project with a large urban school district in another province. The project, entitled On-line Professional Development for Educators Network (OPEN), was funded by the national Office of Learning Technologies, with in-kind contributions from two universities and two school boards. Actual commencement of the project occurred at the same time as the superintendent assumed his position. The goals of the project were as follows: to support the professional development of k-12 educators across Canada to integrate education technology in all areas of the curriculum; to support management of educational change using ICT at classroom, school, district, provincial, and national levels through ICT professional development (PD); and to facilitate improved student achievement. There were six specific project objectives: develop professional learning environments that promote collaboration in rural and urban settings, support implementation of ICT in classrooms and schools (as part of school improvement efforts), provide opportunities for professional collaboration and problem solving to support successful application of models in various contexts (rural and urban) in different parts of Canada, provide PD resources (models, classroom approaches, and assessment tools) that can be used by teachers to integrate technology, build capacity with the partner organizations that can provide leadership and expertise for further expansion, and conduct and disseminate research that demonstrates how ICT facilitates learning and change within a rural or urban educational community (students, teachers, preservice interns, administrators, faculties of education, parents, and private sector).

My Voice

Having been part of the critical friends research team in Discovery School District, I was keenly aware that in spite of the district's efforts to bring about change in the district's schools and classrooms, results were disappointing. While each of the initiatives described above may have contributed to educators' professional learning throughout the district, their impact appeared to be minimal. I assumed the role of superintendent of education at a point in time when we, the critical friends, were beginning to recognize that each of the research and development initiatives in which we had been engaged was occurring as an isolated project that lacked sustainability beyond the end of project funding and therefore was likely to have little districtwide long-term impact. For instance, an internal assessment report of the Learning Village Project two years following its adoption revealed that the level of school and community connectivity and parent and teacher use of the Internet was insufficient to continue with the project. After two years, there was practically no interschool collaboration or communication through the Internet with parents or the community. This led me to conclude at the time that "This is a wonderful product with great potential; however, I think we have purchased a snow blower to mow the lawn."

Adopting a New Approach to Professional Development

Having been a member of the Provincial Advisory Committee on the Coordination of Professional Development and having reviewed the existing literature related to professional development, I realized the necessity of altering the approach to professional development within the district. Consequently, in my opening address as superintendent of education to school principals and program specialists, I committed to working with district personnel to improve professional development within the district. I noted that,

> In spite of the importance placed on professional development, there remains little positive support for the traditional models of one-day in-services or workshops that are held at a district or provincial level. Equally, the evidence related to the impact of professional development on the classroom and the teaching and learning is less than impressive. (Superintendent's opening address to school principals and program specialists)

Further, drawing on the evidence related to successful professional development and personal mastery (Senge et al., 1994), I stated that while professional development is critical to school success, it must be job embedded and driven by individual teacher-identified needs in the context of the priority learning targets that arise from the school's shared vision with considerations given to personal needs, professional requirements, teaching assignments, new courses/curriculum initiatives, the school development plan, and the district strategic education plan. Also, I emphasized that it must be student focused. Therefore, the priority for professional development must be placed on supporting individual teachers in a continuing quest to improve their teaching and learning practices.

In order to initiate change in existing professional development practices, I sought the support of the Administrative Council and GAC to create a new program specialist position for personal and professional learning. This person would lead the development and implementation of a new empirically based professional development approach that was based on principles that had been articulated in a 1998 report of the Provincial Advisory Committee on the Coordination of Professional Development that had been established by the Department of Education but resulted "in little or no action at the provincial level" (Sheppard, 2008, p. 9). Within six months of his appointment, the new program specialist, with the support of a district team of professionals that included teachers, principals, and other program specialists, had developed a model of personal professional learning that redefined both professional development and professional personnel evaluation practices. The latter evaluation processes now focused on professional learning, rather than on the all too typical perfunctory top-down accountability-driven assessment that had previously been the case. GAC accepted the new personal and professional learning model, and implementation began in year two of my tenure. The new personal professional learning program adopted by the district was founded upon the existing best practices and emerging empirical literature (Garet et al., 2001; Glickman et al., 2007; Guskey, 2005; Joyce & Calhoun, 1994; Loucks-Horsley, 1994; Smylie, 1996; Sparks & Hirsh, 1997) and was driven by teacher-identified needs that were articulated in personal professional growth plans. These growth plans were an essential component of the revised professional development model in the district as it required that all teachers develop an annual personal-professional learning plan in collaboration with formal school leaders (such as lead teachers, department heads, or school principals) and altered the model of accountability in respect to personal professional learning.

In the past, all teachers were held accountable for attendance at professional development sessions. The approach was based on the assumption that training was synonymous with changed practice and that experts were someone other than teachers. It held teachers accountable for attendance at training sessions, but teachers were not held accountable for their learning or for any follow-up action as a result of that learning. The reality, of course, was that teachers decided whether they would implement the change (Glickman et al., 2007; Guskey, 2000; Hall & Hord, 2006; Hargreaves & Evans, 1997). In the newly implemented model, teachers were accountable, in consultation with the formal leaders (principal, vice principal, department heads, and/or district personnel), to decide what professional development they needed in order to implement curriculum and instructional changes necessary to foster student learning in the context of provincial, district, and school policies, goals, and objectives. Each teacher determined his/her priority needs, and the school leaders and district program staff attempted to facilitate delivery on these articulated needs. The district and school boards were accountable for the provision of an adequate level of support and the required resources for individual's learning experience, while the professional learner committed to sharing new knowledge with district colleagues and, where applicable, the utilization of that knowledge to improve school and classroom conditions in support of student learning (DiBella, Nevis, & Gould, 1996). A valued component of the professional learning experiences supported by the district was learning from external sources. In support of this, the district established a professional development fund to support annually a select number of principals, program specialists, and teachers to attend national or international conferences in support of their professional learning goals.

While we were implementing a new approach to professional development in Discovery School District, a Ministerial Panel on Educational Delivery in the Classroom was in the process of examining the education system in order to advise the minister of education on ways to advance the classroom reform process and to address the outstanding issues of improvement and effective program delivery. Their report, Supporting Learning (Williams & Sparks, 2000), created a multiagency committee, the Professional Development Alliance, which was tasked with developing a new collaborative framework for teacher professional development. Both Brown and I were invited to be founding members of this Alliance. While we were instrumental in shaping the Alliance professional development model, our engagement as Alliance members also contributed to a reshaping of the new Dis-

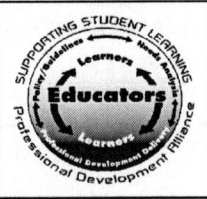

Elaborations
Professional development is the continual renewal of personal knowledge and expertise that leads to improved professional competence in support of student learning. Professional development engages individuals and groups in a broad range of teacher activities including teacher preparation, in-service, individual development, program implementation, staff development, and organizational development.
Educators refer primarily to teachers but also include professional personnel at school districts, the Department of Education, Memorial University and the Newfoundland and Labrador Teachersf Association.
Learners refer to both educators and students, all of whom are engaged in lifelong learning and who continually learn from one another in a variety of ways.
Supporting Student Learning: All professional development is focused on enhancing student learning.
Policy/Guidelines include definitions, beliefs and best practices that impact on professional development in the province. Policies and guidelines also refer to frameworks and procedures for recognizing participation in professional development. Each educator determines his or her PD needs in the context of policy/guidelines and other inputs. Inputs, both internal and external, refer to those forces that drive the need for professional development activities, including new curricula, the findings of research into aspects of teaching and learning, policies and regulations, strategic plans, social and economic conditions and individual professional growth plans.
Needs Analysis refers to such activities as setting annual agendas, monitoring the impact of professional development initiatives and highlighting particular areas of need, both organizational and individual.
Providers. Providers include the individuals, groups and mechanisms through whom or which professional developmental activities are undertaken. Providers can be internal or external to the province or the education system. Within the provincial education system, PD providers include teachers, program specialists/consultants/officers (District, Department of Education, NLTA), Special Interest Councils of NLTA, Memorial University, the Centre for Distance Learning and Innovation (CDLI) and the NLTA Virtual Teacher Centre (VTC).
Forms of PD. Forms of PD include the various ways professional development can be organized and delivered, including institutes, workshops, learning teams and individualized learning. These forms of PD may be undertaken face to face, through mediating technologies (e.g. web-based), private study, or combinations of various types.

Fig. 6.1 Professional Development Alliance Model

covery School District model during its early stages of implementation. In the final analysis, when the new model for professional development was adopted as the provincial model for professional development (see Fig. 6.1) through the work of the Provincial Professional Development Alliance, Discovery School District was in its third year of implementation.

This new model of professional development was essential to improved professional learning throughout the district, but GAC believed that without a specific focus on improving classroom practices, it might do little more than provide improved learning opportunities for teachers without having any meaningful impact on what they do in the classroom or on student learning. It was toward that purpose that GAC engaged in the development of a shared vision for teaching and learning as described in Chapter 5. We (GAC) believed that such a vision would help the entire organization and individuals within it to focus their personal-professional learning goals on continuous improvement of their classroom practices.

While I have no empirical evidence that the professional development initiatives that were focused on achieving the shared vision of teaching and learning (outlined in Chapter 5) contributed to improved classroom practices or student learning, there are a number of indicators that suggest a trend in a positive direction. Over the span of a four-year period, there was an 11% increase in the extent to which teachers perceived that their school had a vision statement that guided their actions, a 13% increase in teachers' perceptions that there was a clear plan for moving toward their vision, and a 27% increase in the extent to which individual teachers perceived that their colleagues were committed to improvements in teaching and learning (Sheppard & Brown, 2007).

A second indicator of how the shared vision of teaching and learning influenced teachers' professional learning plans relates to the use of ICT in support of student learning. Because classroom use of ICT in support of student learning was identified as a component of the vision for teaching and learning, a large number of teachers identified it as a personal professional learning goal. Because the skill levels of those identifying this as a learning goal varied, the district brought together a leadership team of program specialists and lead teachers in this field to develop and implement a professional development plan to meet the needs of teachers at three skill levels: beginner, intermediate, and advanced. Essential to the plan were follow-up activities and supports that assisted early users to build on their initial professional development experience (Discovery School Board, *Annual Report*, 2002–2003). Recognizing that there were few examples of best practices in the classroom use of ICT to support student learning within the district, the district established a series of professional learning centers. These centers were established at each level of schooling (primary, elementary, intermediate, and high school) and in one categorical and one non-categorical special education class. The lead teachers for these learning centers assumed responsibility to develop, pilot, and document through a written innovation profile best practices in the use of ICT as a classroom tool focused on holistic learning, reflective problem-solving exercises, collaborative grouping, and social interactions that promote higher-order thinking and meaningful learning. Moreover, they archived resources for the purpose of having a digital repository that could be shared by others. The resources and innovative profile of best practices were made available to those teachers who were in the early-use stages (Hall and Hord, 2006) in the adoption of ICT as a classroom tool. In the first year, the centers were a huge success as suggested by the following comment by a special education teacher who was an early user:

> The students have improved and learned more in one month than they had in years. Integration obviously works, and my colleagues are right on the bandwagon! Again, Thanks! We couldn't have done it without you guys. (Discovery School District, *Annual Report*, 2002–2003).

As for improvements in student learning, province-wide tests in grades 3, 6, 9, and 12 revealed that the district experienced rapid improvement in scores at all levels as documented in the following excerpt from correspondence from the deputy minister of education to the chairperson of the school board:

> It is clear the efforts your board had made to improve student achievement is paying off, as is evidenced in the district's improved criterion referenced test (CRT) and public examination results in 2002–03. As you know, this trend is continuing, as [this year's] ... scores indicate [the district] has once again produced excellent results. (deputy minister of education, personal communication, October 15, 2003)

DISCOVERY SCHOOL BOARD PRESS RELEASE

A recent national report on the **Quality of Public Education in Canada** published by the Learning Partnership states that, "When it comes to figuring out a math problem or writing a report, Canadian students rank among the world's best."

This being the case, parents of students in Discovery School District should certainly be excited about the most recent provincial assessment results:

- Discovery Grade 3 students performed the highest in the province in language arts.
- Discovery Grade 6 students performed the highest in the province in language arts.
- Discovery Grade 6 students performed the highest in the province in mathematics.
- Discovery Grade 9 students performed the highest in the province in reading, mathematics, and science.
- Discovery Grade 9 students performed above the provincial average in 6 of 7 areas of French.
- Discovery Senior High students performed above the provincial average on 10 of 11 public examination courses and performed as well as the provincial average on the eleventh.

Board Chairperson, Carol stated, "The Board is ecstatic about the latest achievement results! Just a few years ago, students in Discovery School District achieved average results in respect to students in other school districts in this Province. Overall, they are now leading the way."

Fig. 6.2 Student achievement press release

Also, the extent of the improvement in comparison to other school districts in the same province was outlined in a school board press release (see Fig. 6.2). Unfortunately, the full potential of the new professional development approach in Discovery School District is difficult to assess as it became a victim of government restructuring (see Chapter 7) during the year following the completion of the shared vision.

Through the Lens of Critical Friends

It appears that our early research/professional development partnership initiatives related to leadership for the implementation of the district's ICT agenda helped build the capacity related to the use of ICT for teaching and learning within the district. Furthermore, the links to the university appeared to help keep the district informed on recent research and trends, and their active involvement in research raised their awareness of possibilities and what was happening in other Canadian jurisdictions; new software and hardware created excitement about the new possibilities. In spite of those positive aspects, we were somewhat disappointed that these initiatives did not lead to more district-wide sustainable changes in teaching and learning. Fortunately, our partnership with the district continued, and we were able to participate in the development of a new empirically based professional development approach focused on improving teaching and learning throughout the entire district.

The implementation of the district's new model of professional development was not without its challenges, however. Because the new model was based on professional choice, there was a great deal of resistance from some program specialists who had normally decided what was important for teachers to learn. There was resistance at the provincial level, as well, as the Department of Education consultants began to realize that the district was no longer willing to mandate that teachers attend training sessions that external sources (such as those at the Department of Education) felt necessary. The district was able to overcome the provincial resistance by securing the support of the deputy minister of education. As reported in Chapter 4, resistance from program specialists began to evaporate as members began to recognize that the new approach resulted in improved professional learning, improved programming, and increases in student achievement.

A significant threat to the success of the district's implementation of the professional development model resulted from a misinterpretation of "professional choice" by a newly hired assistant superintendent of human resources. She approved one teacher's request to engage in a costly training program that had no apparent connection to his teaching duties, but was focused on one of the key goals of the district to promote healthy living. The teacher was in his last year before retirement eligibility and used the opportunity to train at the board's expense for a new job outside of the organization. This gap in the district accountability system further eroded support for the new professional development model and dictated detailed clarification of personal mastery, personal and professional growth, and professional development to ensure that the purposes of the district were well served. Upon reflection, it reveals the challenges of bringing clarity to new initiatives during the implementation stage. Also, willingness to admit that this gap existed without serious reprisal for the decision-maker demonstrated the organization's tolerance for failure related to risk taking. This encouraged others to take measured risks and not to hide inherent failures or mistakes, but to treat them as learning experiences (Kouzes & Posner, 2003).

A second threat to the district's new approach to professional development resulted from the government's continued reduction in the level of funding for professional development to all school districts. In spite of this reduction to an already lean budget and the board's focus on reducing a large accumulated budget deficit, the school board believed that professional development for teachers and principals was important and worth fighting for. They became more focused on teaching and learning and had come to recognize the importance of teacher professional development as well. For instance, a trustee indicated that he was delighted that the district had produced videos highlighting exemplary teaching practices. In his view, this was one of the most significant professional development initiatives the district had taken in his term in office as he saw it as modeling the type of teaching that was expected. He observed that the school board had become more focused on teaching and learning and had become more supportive of teacher professional development. Moreover, it is noteworthy that the importance of professional development as a means of improving student learning was noted in each of the board's annual reports during that period and the trustee boasted that in spite of government cuts to the professional development budget, "we made it a line item in our budget and when things got tight we fought to keep it there, and so far we have succeeded" (Brown, Dibbon, & Sheppard, 2003).

While teachers remained highly critical of the inadequate level of funding for professional development, it appears that they may have recognized the school board's commitment to it in the face of declining resources. During this period, the percentage of teachers who perceived that the organization supported them in the achievement of their personal professional goals rose by 25% over a four-year period (Sheppard & Brown, 2006).

Leithwood (1996) has argued for central policy initiatives that define expected outcomes, but at the same time allow schools to develop the learning capacity to determine their own processes and implementation strategies. In spite of the district's new approach to professional development, it is not surprising that schools were not anxious to assume this role as most continued to work within the mindscapes of the traditional model (where program specialists decided the professional development program), and it is likely that principals were not confident that they could make these decisions either. Their engagement in the development of a decision matrix for teaching and learning (see Figs. 4.4 and 4.5), their engagement in the development of the shared vision for teaching and learning, and the school's ownership of the school-level implementation and decisions related to teacher professional development proved to be effective strategies in overcoming these mindscapes. It clarified the role of principals (and the school) in determining what professional development was needed, who would be involved, and how it would contribute to meaningful changes in classroom practices. It demonstrated as well that district personnel had roles to play that were supportive of schools, rather than as agents of top-down accountability. This was particularly evident in respect to the locally developed videos that provided images of the teaching and learning vision in practice, provided a celebration of current practice, and highlighted for individual schools, principals, and teachers that they were members of a family of schools through which they could both contribute to and draw strength from the entire district.

As a result of the redefined roles of program specialists who now worked as partners and boundary spanners between schools, families of schools, and schools and the school district, the professional learning capacity was enhanced. For example, one program specialist brought together a team of lead teachers to develop learning experiences for teachers in the use of ICT as part of their teaching and learning repertoire. Within a two-year period, nearly every school in the district had two learning centers that served as centers of excellence for the use of ICT in support of student learning. These centers were available as professional learning centers for teachers and thereby contributed to increased teacher capacity for the use of ICT in the classroom. Beyond the expectation that increased teacher capacity would improve classroom practices, there was an unanticipated direct impact on student learning. Many of the district's schools were in rural regions where students traveled long distances by school bus. While teachers provided regular tutorial sessions, many students could not avail of them because of their home location. As a result of the developing expertise of lead teachers in the ICT professional learning centers, several of them designed multimedia learning clips that provided tutorial learning experiences that all students could access at home. These learning clips became so successful they became a model for schools throughout the entire province.

While we did not collect data that would allow us to confirm that either the shared vision of teaching and learning or the new approach to professional development made a positive difference to classroom practices and student learning, the anecdotal evidence and our general observations as participant observers in support of that view is compelling. Among the most compelling of our observations was the excitement and energy that we observed among the teachers and various other participants during the inaugural screening of each of the k-6 and 7-12 classroom practices videos.

References

Borko, H. (2004). Professional development and teacher learning: Mapping the terrain. *Educational Researcher, 33* (8), 3–15.

Brown, J., Dibbon, D., & Sheppard, B. (2003, May). *The school trustee in a learning environment.* Paper presented at the Annual Conference of CSSE, Halifax, Nova Scotia, Canada.

DiBella, A. J., Nevis, E. C., & Gould, J. M. (1996). Understanding organizational learning capacity. *Journal of Management Studies, 33*(3), 361–379.

Elmore, R. (2002). *Bridging the gap between standards and achievement: The imperative for professional development in education.* Washington, DC: Albert Shanker Institute.

Fullan, M. (2001). *Leading in a culture of change.* San Francisco, CA: Jossey-Bass.

Garet, M., Porter, A., Desimone, L., Birman, B., & Suk Yoon, K. (2001). What makes professional development effective? Results from a national sample of teachers. *American Educational Research Journal, 38*(4), 915–945.

Glickman, C., Gordon, S., & Ross-Gordon, J. (2007). *SuperVision of instructional leadership: A developmental approach.* Needham Heights, MA: Allyn & Bacon.

Guskey, T. (2000). *Evaluating professional development.* Thousand Oaks, CA: Corwin.

Guskey, T. (2005). Taking a second look. *Journal of Staff Development, 26*(1), 10–18.

Hall, G., & Hord, S. (2006). *Implementing change: Patterns, principles, and potholes.* Toronto, ON: Pearson Education.

Hargreaves, A., & Evans, R. (1997). Teachers and educational reform. In A. Hargreaves & R. Evans (Eds.). *Beyond educational reform: Bringing teachers back in* (pp. 1–18). Philadelphia, PA: Open University Press.

Joyce, B., & Calhoun, E. (1994). Staff development: Advances in the last twenty-five years in "Reflections on 25 years of staff development." *Journal of Staff Development, 15*(4), 3–4.

Kouzes, J., & Posner, B. (2003). *Credibility.* San Francisco, CA: Jossey-Bass.

Leithwood, K. (1996). Commitment-building approaches to school restructuring: Lessons from a longitudinal study. *Journal of Educational Policy, 2*(3), 377–398.

Leithwood, K., & Jantzi, D. (2005). *A review of transformational school leadership research 1996–2005.* Paper presented at the annual meeting of the American Educational Research Association, Montreal, Canada.

Liebeman, A. (1995). *The work of restructuring schools.* New York: Teachers College Press.

Loucks-Horsley, S. (1994). Significant advancements in staff development in the past 25 years. *Journal of Staff Development, 15*(4), 7–8.

Louis, K.S. (2007). *Changing the culture of schools: Professional community, organizational learning and trust.* Paper presented at Teacher Working Conditions that Matter: The Symposium. Elementary Teachers Federation of Ontario: Toronto, ON, Canada.

Penuel, W., Fishman, B., Yamaguchi, R., & Gallagher, L. (2007). What makes professional development effective? Strategies that foster curriculum implementation. *American Educational Research Journal, 44*(4), pp. 921–958.
Ryan, J. (2006). *Inclusive leadership*. San Francisco, CA: Jossey-Bass.
Schlechty, P. (2001). *Shaking up the school house*. San Francisco: Jossey-Bass.
Senge, P., Roberts, C., Ross, R., Smith, B., & Kleiner, A. (1994). *The fifth discipline fieldbook*. Toronto: Doubleday.
Sheppard, B. (1996). Exploring the transformational nature of instructional leadership. *Alberta Journal of Educational Research, 42*(4), 325–344.
Sheppard, B. (2008). *Professional development practices in Newfoundland and Labrador*. St. John's, NL, Canada: Virtual Teachers Centre: Retrieved September 28, 2008 from http://www.virtualteachercentre.ca/ken/documents/CCL-Paper.pdf.
Sheppard, B., & Brown, J. (2006, October). *A CEO's five year journey: Translating theory into practice*. Paper presented at Commonwealth Council for Educational Administration and Management, Nicosia, Cyprus.
Sheppard, B., & Brown, J. (2007, April). *The CEO as an emergent leader in a school district hierarchy: Challenges and opportunities*. Paper presented at American Educational Research Association, Chicago.
Smylie, M. (1996). From bureaucratic control to building human capital: the importance of teacher learning in education reform. *Educational Researcher, 25* (9), 9–11.
Sparks, D., & Hirsh, S. (1997). *A new vision for staff development*. Oxford, OH: Association for Supervision and Curriculum Development.
Starratt, R. (2004). *Ethical leadership*. San Francisco, CA: Jossey-Bass.
Williams, L., & Sparks, R. (2000). *Supporting learning: A report of the Ministerial Panel on the educational delivery in the classroom*. St. John's, NL: Government of Newfoundland and Labrador.

Chapter 7
Systems Challenges to Growth and Sustainability of Meaningful Educational Reform

Abstract Effective school districts function as complex adaptive learning organizations that work with multiple partners to mitigate the varied systemic factors that frequently inhibit student learning. This chapter reveals the challenges and successes of a school district that experienced considerable success functioning in this manner. The district was even able to overcome most of the challenges imposed by the traditional hierarchical bureaucratic controls of government; however, in the final analysis, sustainability of meaningful reform was largely dependent on long-term government support.

As we have established in previous chapters, most observers of the school systems in the Western world conclude that educational reform is challenging, and as a consequence, the most significant elements of today's schools remain the same as they were throughout the second half of the previous century. For the most part, teachers still operate in isolation from one another; they deliver content to students, use paper-and-pencil tests to determine how much information students have retained at a particular point in time, and use the accumulated results of these tests across a number of subject areas to determine whether a student passes or fails and how well she/he has done in comparison to her/his peers. Having observed the apparent intransigence of school systems to change, we share Elmore's (2002) view that "the existing structure and culture of schools seem better designed to resist learning and improvement than to enable it" (p. 4).

While we accept the view that reform efforts have not done much to change schools and that the existing structures and culture perpetuate the status quo, we do not accept contentions that teachers and educational administrators are to blame for this reality. Rather, we believe that change has not occurred because most educational reform efforts have been simplistic, externally imposed solutions that have been either poorly designed or inadequately implemented. For the most part, educational reform has focused on dealing with single factors and political "quick-fixes" that fail to address the complexities and systemic nature of the problems in the public education system and "what takes place in classrooms" (Knapp, 1997, p. 227). We concur with Emery (2006) who suggests that it appears that would-be reformers repeatedly have "understated how hard it is to get from here to there" (p. xi) and who contends that little meaningful sustained change in education is likely to be achieved without the recognition that "education is a system, not a collection of parts" (p. 2). Frequently, inadequate attention is given to implementation of the reform initiative and its systemic nature. As a result, only a select few—the innovators and leaders—become engaged in it, while the majority give it superficial attention as they await the introduction of yet another fad. This typical simplistic approach to reform that is based on a naïve assumption that adoption is synonymous with implementation, in our view, is a primary reason for the lack of sustainability of change initiatives. If implementation efforts fail to go beyond the introduction of a reform initiative, asking why that initiative has not been sustained is irrelevant because there has been no reform to sustain!

Toward Meaningful School Reform

Throughout this book, we have argued that in response to the well-documented failure of school reform, there has been a growing body of empirical evidence that has fueled support for the importance of organizational learning as a promising approach for bringing about meaningful, sustained improvement in schools and school systems (Fullan, 2005; Giles & Hargreaves, 2006; Hall & Hord, 2006; Leithwood, Louis, Anderson, & Wahlstrom, 2004). Employing an organizational learning framework requires recognition that schools are just one component of a complex adaptive learning system that is composed of multiple dynamic interrelated subsystems that interact to influence student learning. Fullan (2005) and Sackney (2007) suggest that there are three primary sources of formal leadership that must work together in order for school systems to function as professional learning communities: schools, districts, and government. Figure 7.1 (a slightly modified version of the leadership framework by Leithwood et al.) recognizes these three leadership sources and identifies how they interact with other stakeholders and multiple variables to influence student learning. Critical to the understanding of this framework is the assumption that the relationships among the variables in the framework are interdependent and complex and that each variable potentially directly and indirectly impacts other variables that either facilitate or inhibit student learning. For instance, school leaders influence and are influenced by provincial/state government; district leadership; other stakeholder groups such as unions, professional associations, community and business groups, federal government, the judicial system, and the media; and multiple professional learning experiences. In spite of the interdependence of each of these leadership sources, each independently, either directly or indirectly, influences school and classroom conditions and student learning. For example, the Youth Criminal Justice Act and related Supreme Court rulings (Mackay & Sutherland, 2006; R. v. A.M., 2008) have had major implications for Canadian schools, and some parents and educators believe that both have made it much more difficult to maintain safe schools as they argue that the balance has tipped too far in favor of individual freedom rather than student safety

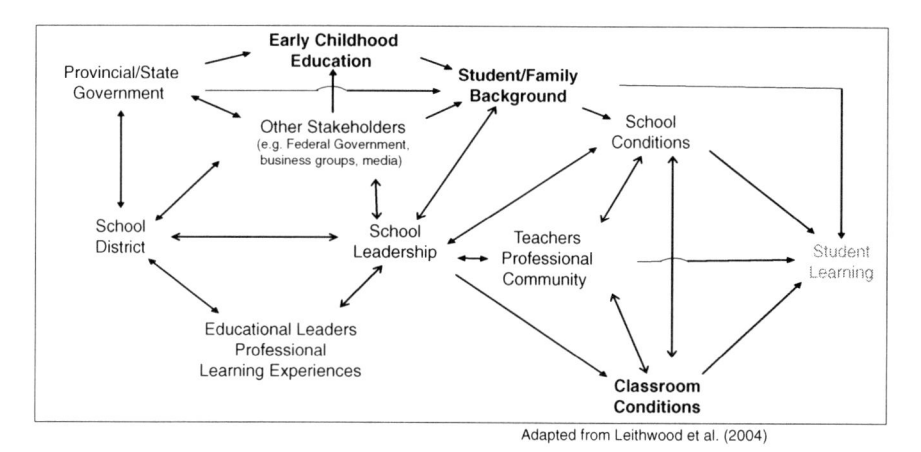

Fig. 7.1 Linking leadership to learning

(Johnson, 2008). Aside from the fact that student safety is independently of utmost importance, it is a school condition that directly impacts student learning (Ma, 2002). If students do not feel safe, they are unlikely to be focused on learning.

Among the most recognized and well-established influences on student learning are factors related to student and family background. These factors have been found to account for more than 50% of the variance in student achievement outcomes (Harris, Chapman, Muijs, Russ, & Stoll, 2006; Kohn, 2002; Stoll & Fink, 1996). For instance, in a recent study of intermediate students (Atlantic Evaluation and Research Consultants, 2008), we found that two background factors commonly used as measures of socioeconomic status (CMEC, 2007, 2008b)—mother's education level and the number of books in the home—were associated with huge differences in students' post-secondary aspirations: 31% fewer students with mothers having less than high-school education and 40% fewer students who have very few books in the home indicated that they aspire to getting a post-secondary education in comparison to the those who are most advantaged in these respects. Fortunately, however, as indicated in Fig. 7.1, there is some evidence that the negative impact of family background factors that limit students' ability to learn can be somewhat mitigated by school leadership (Harris et al.) and by social policies designed to support families and communities (Ungerleider, 2003). Ungerleider argues that social policies that include "decent minimum wages, generous parenting policies, universal day care and early-childhood education, fair employment standards, and health care" (pp. 294–295) are required if society is to expect meaningful improvement in student learning in public schools. It is obvious that government leadership is required if any of those social policies are to become a reality.

School leaders may be able to mitigate the negative impact of the family and community factors by providing direct school support to the family and through efforts to engage the larger community in providing supports. However, direct school support to families is difficult to provide in a system that has been typically resource challenged and where school leaders are notoriously overburdened. Furthermore, some argue that mobilizing the larger community in support of public k-12 education in an increasingly fast-paced, self-centered world may be somewhat idealistic and perhaps even naïve.

Beyond the direct impact of family and community background on student learning, Knapp (1997) offers another perspective of how families and other members of the larger school community impact efforts to bring about school and classroom reform. He suggests that in final analysis

> perhaps, the most problematic thing that intervenes between reform and the classroom is the degree to which the public (a) perceives good things to be happening in ... classrooms and (b) is willing to give the reforms time to demonstrate how far reaching the resulting improvements might be. (p. 259)

No doubt, public perceptions have considerable impact on the decision-making among political leaders (government or district trustees) who need to demonstrate results prior to the next election (Galway, 2008). If the electorate perceives a new program or an initiative is less than positive, in all likelihood it will become an election issue or may even be dropped before an election is called.

Within the context of their more traditional in-school leadership role (e.g., instructional leadership), school leaders influence the schools' ability to learn, thereby impacting school and classroom conditions and teachers' professional commitment, professional engagement, and openness to be innovative (Sheppard, 1996) that have been found to be associated with improved student outcomes (Hallinger & Heck, 1999; Hanushek, 2004; Mulford, Silins, & Leithwood, 2004). As for the impact of teachers on student learning, the evidence is convincing that "individual teachers have a powerful effect on students' academic achievement" (Hill & Flynn, 2006; Marzano, Pickering, & Pollock, 2001). Knapp (1997) draws attention to the important role of teachers in bringing about educational reform as he argues that the success of any reform initiative is ultimately dependent on "what teachers themselves internalize as the operative standard to which they hold themselves accountable" (p. 257). If this is indeed the case, there is little doubt that the meaningful engagement of teachers in the educational reform process is essential.

Given the complex, systemic nature of the multiple factors that impact student learning as noted above, it is readily apparent that any expectation that any one group or agency can identify and impose solutions to mitigate the impact of all of those factors is unrealistic and naïve. Our argument is that meaningful sustained educational reform will occur in schools only through collaborative leadership and organizational learning that is systemic and adaptive and that engages the multiple sources of leadership of each of the interrelated subsystems in purposeful interaction focused on improving student learning.

As noted in Chapter 3, we believe that the school district has the most potential for fostering such large-scale systemic reform; however, long-term success is highly unlikely "if the larger system [and in particular government] is not a partner in fostering the sustainability agenda" (Fullan, 2005, p. 80). In the next section we will explore some examples of how Discovery School District interacted with the major system partners and how the district was influenced by these partners and how it attempted to influence them.

Systems Thinking in Discovery School District

The federal government has no formal jurisdiction over k-12 education in Canada. However, laws related to children and youth as well as special federal programs targeted at youth employment, regional economic development, second-language programs, and the development of the national communications and technology infrastructure have had a huge impact on school districts such as Discovery School District. For instance, Discovery School District benefited greatly from various federal programs. By working in partnership with other local agencies (e.g., Regional Economic Development Boards), Discovery School District accessed many federal government programs offered through Human Resources and Development Canada (HRDC) and Industry Canada. As a result of funding and human resource support provided by these federal government agencies over the course of a decade, the district championed improved connectivity to the district's schools, private homes, local businesses, and agencies throughout the entire geographic region served by the school district. The programs brought computer hardware and software into the schools along with several hundred highly skilled support personnel, and they provided learning opportunities that built the capacity of teachers, parents, students, and the general public in using ICT for learning, business development and communication (e.g., Discovery School Board, *Annual Report*, 2003). Moreover, with the support of the provincial Federation of School Councils, Discovery School Board was able to avail of a federal program that directly targeted meaningful parental involvement in the life and education of students in their early adolescence as a means of reducing risk factors and improving learning outcomes for children from challenging socioeconomic circumstances (Discovery School Board, *Annual Report*, 2003).

In recognition of the negative impact of low socioeconomic conditions on children's educational success, Discovery School District was committed to actions to mitigate these negative forces. While predecessor school districts together with other social agencies had lobbied both the provincial and federal governments for the establishment of early childhood education programs, it had resulted in little action. Therefore, shortly after Discovery School District was founded in the mid-1990s, it established its own early childhood intervention program for preschool children. Because early childhood education was beyond the mandate of the school district, however, it was more challenging to access external resources to support the program. Nevertheless, the district persevered, and as a result of the successes of their early intervention program over a six-year period, the provincial government adopted the program for the entire province. Clearly, this is one example of how school districts can influence provincial directions rather than to be just passive recipients of top-down mandates. As a result of its leadership, Discovery School

District impacted learning opportunities for children throughout the entire province at the same time as they benefitted from the additional resources and financial supports that accompanied the provincial implementation of the early intervention program.

In addition to the early intervention program for preschool children, district program specialists for primary education and literacy held a number of sessions with parents of preschool children throughout the district. These sessions focused primarily on the importance of reading and language development and the need for direct parent involvement in their children's education. Moreover, district personnel engaged school councils in a conversation about the importance of early childhood intervention and encouraged them to support community-based preschool initiatives. The district recognized that in spite of their efforts focused on overcoming the typical learning deficits of low socioeconomic conditions, many children would arrive at school less well prepared than others that were more socially and economically advantaged. Given this recognition, the district committed to "the development of a k-12 literacy plan with increased emphasis on reading and writing interventions for k-4 students" (Discovery School Board, *Strategic Plan*, 2004) to optimize the likelihood that all children, with the exception of those with profound learning exceptionalities, would be reading at grade level.

Also, the superintendent became involved as a provincial and national advocate for the recognition that socioeconomic factors and the extent to which the student's community and family value education have considerable impact on school and classroom conditions and individual student achievement. In this advocacy role, through several national forums, he challenged provincial governments for their increased emphasis on test scores in specific subjects and condemned right-wing think tanks for their ranking of schools based on student scores on these tests, with little consideration of these aforementioned wider social conditions (Sheppard, 2001, 2002, 2004).

In spite of the considerable leadership exercised by Discovery School District as it attempted to engage multiple sources of leaders to influence the varied factors that impact on student learning, in the final analysis, government control presented huge challenges to the sustainability of its reform agenda. In the remainder of this chapter, we explore several of these larger system challenges.

Systems Challenges to the Discovery School District Reform Agenda

Challenge 1: Government Control of Financial and Human Resources

Discovery School District was funded entirely by government. Teachers, district educational personnel, and senior administrators were paid directly by government, and the remaining budget was allocated to the school board as a grant with specifically designated components (as opposed to block funding) as follows: instruction, repairs and maintenance, school secretarial, maintenance wages, and operations. For the most part, government expected school boards to allocate the resources by components in similar proportions to that which they received. A particular challenging aspect of government's approach to budgeting for school boards was the government's total control of capital expenditures and the reduction of the budget allocation for repair and maintenance. During the mid-1990s, as government became increasingly obsessed with reducing the provincial debt, capital spending in education was drastically reduced. Also, the funding for repair, maintenance, and cleaning was reduced from a rate of $0.96 to $0.55 per square foot as a cost-cutting measure, and it remained at that lower rate for more than a decade following. An additional challenge related to this reduction in the repairs and maintenance budget was the escalating costs of servicing the growing emerging technology infrastructure (the purchase of which was largely funded through school-level fundraising). Because there was no special budget allocation either to employ computer technology support specialists or to purchase hardware, all school districts in the province, including Discovery School District, were forced to reduce already underfunded support staff allocations (school secretarial and custodial) in order to provide at least minimal essential service in this emerging area (Warren, Curtis, Sheppard, Hillier, & Roberts, 2003).

Given these circumstances, the Discovery School Board was restricted in its ability to purchase cleaning and maintenance supplies and to enter into preventative maintenance contracts. This led to a deterioration of many school facilities that over the course of a decade resulted in leaking roofs and windows and the build-up of dust and mould. In such circumstances, considerable time and effort was spent in crisis management, lobbying government for more resources, and restructuring school systems in order to eliminate those buildings that posed the greatest safety threat or health hazard to their occupants. In spite of those challenges, Discovery School District was able to improve its external performance rating for occupational health and safety by 50%. While this was something to celebrate given the challenging circumstances, in reality, the improvements occurred because of the considerable priority that was given to it by school board trustees, district and school personnel, and parents. While we applaud the focus on the safety and comfort of students and school personnel, we are convinced that the challenges presented by the inadequate level of funding necessitated an inordinate effort to achieve this safety goal that diverted attentions away from a collective focus on improving teaching and learning processes.

In addition to controlling school board funding, the government maintained control of the allocation of classroom teachers, guidance counselors, student support specialists, and school administrators through the use of a school-based formula. Throughout the period of our study, Discovery School District experienced a rapid decline in student population, and as a result the existing bureaucratic formula approach to allocating teachers by school created multiple challenges related to program delivery in small schools and contributed to large class sizes in larger schools (Shortall & Greene-Fraize, 2007). While the school district had some flexibility in teacher assignment to individual schools, removing a teacher unit from a school to which the unit had been allocated through the government formula and assigning it to another school, when both schools were perceived by the school community as understaffed to begin with, proved to be politically challenging. Similarly, the growing demands of information technology created challenges in respect to teacher allocations. Because there was no allocation of information technology teachers, these units were taken from elsewhere. Most commonly, schools replaced the teacher-librarian unit with an information technology resource person that may have negatively impacted both student and teacher learning resource support.

Even more problematic, as noted by the Individual Support Services and Pathways Commission (Langdon & Somerton, 2007), was the control by government of the allocation of categorical special education teachers to schools:

> The overwhelming message gleaned from the ... hearings was that the ISSP [Individual Support Services Plan] and Pathways models resembled a good idea gone awry, a sound concept which has lost its focus (p. 6) .... [And] of equal concern was the approval process for ... applications for categorical service. Once developed, applications are forwarded to the Department of Education for approval. All stakeholders noted the irony in a system of decision making where those who know the child the least, have the final decision over their programming. (p. 54)

Beyond maintaining control of funding and the allocation of all teaching professionals, government held control of labor negotiations for all school district employees as well. While school boards were invited to participate in the negotiations, they had no authority to make decisions. In spite of their lack of power during labor negotiations, they were held entirely responsible for managing any job actions, such as work stoppages or strikes that resulted from them. During the five-year time span of our study of Discovery School District, there were two lengthy general strikes of all support staff including school secretaries, student assistants (for students with special needs), and cleaning and maintenance personnel. During both labor disruptions, schools remained open with the support of essential cleaning services that were provided by a small group of striking workers and supplemented by district management personnel. Teachers were expected to attend to any students with special needs without the support of a student assistant, and school principals were expected to function without the support of administrative assistants (school secretaries). While these labor disruptions (strikes) were not necessarily a direct function of government control, the expectations placed on school district administrators by government during those strikes created long-term challenges to the Discovery School District reform agenda. Beyond disrupting the teaching and learning agenda for several weeks, the engagement of district personnel in managing the strike was detrimental to the district's agenda of increasing collaborative leadership and shared decision-making in order to facilitate organizational learning. As found in other studies (Bryk & Schneider, 2003; Tschannen-Moran & Hoy, 2000), it also negatively impacted staff morale and the level of trust between school and district office personnel.

Challenge 2: The Difficult Transition from Purpose to Practice

While education in Canada is a provincial responsibility and there is no federal ministry of education, the visions and purposes of k-12 education across the country are similar (Atlantic Evaluation and Research Consultants, 2008; CMEC, 1997, 2007, 2008a; Council of Atlantic Ministers of Education and Training [CAMET], n.d.; Western and Northern Canadian Protocol for Collaboration [WNCP], n.d.). In the four Atlantic Provinces, for example, CAMET (n.d.) have agreed to common goals through the articulation of Essential Graduation Learnings that are focused on the following: aesthetic expression, citizenship, communication, personal development, problem solving, and technological competence (e.g., New Brunswick, Department of Education, n.d.). These Essential Graduation Learnings that form the foundation of curriculum and grade-level outcomes of k-12 public education reveal that the articulated purpose in all four of these provinces is to develop culturally literate citizens who are committed to lifelong learning and democratic citizenship, are able to compete in a global economy, and have the capacity for critical thought and the skills and attitudes needed to live in a caring and just society. In addition to those articulated goals, there is an overarching universal recognition in the articulated goals of all schools, school districts, and the provincial departments of education that schools must be safe, caring environments that exist as meaningful social spaces for children and adolescents, rather than as just places to be endured as they prepare for adult life. Within that context, Discovery School Board committed to the following vision statement: "To challenge and develop the learning and achievement capabilities of each student in a safe, caring, and socially just learning environment" (Discovery School District, 2004).

While there are minor variations across Canadian provinces in respect to what Canadians want from the public school system, in general, most want schools to be focused on providing strong foundations in reading, writing, and numeracy and expect them to ensure that their graduates can demonstrate the attainment of an adequate performance level on provincial tests in English language, mathematics, and science and to ensure that they are prepared for post-secondary education and the changing labor market (CMEC, 2008a). Moreover, they expect schools to strengthen common moral values; promote citizenship education and political engagement; promote healthy living; develop social skills and technological competence; develop their abilities in and appreciation of the arts, music, and our cultural heritage; and attend to students' personal development (Canadian Council on Learning, 2007; Ungerleider, 2003).

In spite of an apparent general "motherhood and apple pie" agreement on the overall purpose of k-12 education, there is less agreement in respect to what this purpose looks like in practice, the value assigned to the various aspects of the purpose, and how educational success is measured. Some citizens contend that public schools have become soft and that they are engaged in purposes other than those that are most essential. They emphasize the need to get "back to the basics" and call for increased accountability for the attainment of high standards in science, mathematics, and English language as measured through high stakes tests. This group appears to hold assumptions that one can define the basic purpose, align the curriculum to this purpose, develop high standards for meeting it, construct assessment to measure whether all students meet the standard, and reward or punish schools on the basis of whether their students meet the standard (Brooks & Brooks, 1999). In contrast, others argue vehemently against the "back to the basics" agenda contending that the only meaningful purpose of education can be to develop individuals' desire and ability to be lifelong learners and that what is learned in schools must be authentic and must enable students to learn who they are and how to respond to challenges they will face in order to live a fulfilling life (Littky, 2004; Starratt, 2004). Starratt (2004) argues, for example, that "high-stakes testing shrinks the vision of teachers [and leads to] inauthentic ... superficial learning" (pp. 1–2). This latter group believes that the purpose of education must be on the development of a caring, wise, thinking, responsible citizen who has the resources to contribute to the social and economic welfare of self and others and to the enjoyment of life. Yet other citizens place priority on preparing individuals for the new knowledge economy and on the development of strong generic employability skills that include problem solving abilities, communication skills, computer skills, and interpersonal skills (including the ability to work effectively as part of a team) that can be applied to many different challenges that individuals face (Conference Board of Canada, 2008).

Given the pluralistic context of a democratic society such as Canada, and the multiple constituencies that hold a stake in public education, the complexity of reaching consensus on the level of priority to be placed on the varied and somewhat competing priorities is apparent. Indeed, such agreement may not be possible. While this may be a positive aspect of most democratic societies, it presents a challenge for those responsible for k-12 public education. For instance, in Canada, teachers find themselves confronted on a daily basis with attempting to meet those multiple interests while at the same time they feel compelled to adhere to the narrow expectations imposed by provincial testing regimes that place priority on English language, mathematics, and science (Atlantic Evaluation and Research Consultants, 2008). As a result, some teachers feel compelled to teach only tested topics in designated subject areas and to limit time spent on other areas of the curriculum (Laitsch, 2006). Having observed this phenomenon in the USA, Goodlad (2001) opined that, over the long term, these competing perspectives of educational purpose present an ongoing challenge to sustained meaningful reform as the emphasis shifts according to the dominant social political forces at a particular point in time.

Challenge 3: Localized Education in a Globalized World

Throughout the last decade or so, public schools and school boards in Canada, similar to those in other countries—at least those countries that are members of the Organization for Economic Co-operation and Development (OECD)—have become favored targets of various conservative think tanks (e.g., Atlantic Institute for Market Studies, 2008; Fraser Institute, 2008). Some politicians have targeted the school system also, through popular political platforms of improving schools by legislating higher standards and increasing the accountability of educators to meet those standards (Hargreaves & Fink, 2006; Schlechty, 2005; Starratt, 2004). Also, provincial policies and practices throughout Canada have become increasingly impacted by national and international agendas that appear to be somewhat driven by globalization and the rapidly emerging information and communication technologies (Taylor, Rizvi, Lingard, & Henry, 1997). While these influences are somewhat insidiously imbedded in ongoing social change, the direct observable shifts in provincial policies, structures, and governance appear to be largely influenced by the OECD and the Canadian Council of Ministers of Education (CMEC) as they respond to "the political work of various social movements" (Taylor et al., p. 3). Taylor et al. argue that as "society has become more complex, and interest groups more assertive ... education is no longer discussed in terms of broad visions and ideals but in terms of what governments believe to be possible and often expedient, and what interest groups feel they can persuade governments to do" (p. 3). As a result of such a shift, "education is increasingly regarded as an [economic] commodity, [rather than] a public good" (Shaker & Grimmett, 2004, p. 29). Considered as a commodity, it must be quantified so that the educational assets of a province/state or country can be compared to others. As a consequence, there has been increased accountability in the form of narrowly defined centrally controlled test measures at the expense of authentic learning that is more difficult to quantify.

Consistent with this approach, most provinces in Canada have implemented their own testing program and the ministers of education issue regular press releases touting the success of their education accountability initiatives using test scores as evidence (Shaker & Grimmett, 2004). For Discovery School District, the measures included public examinations at the high-school level and criterion reference tests in mathematics and English language arts in grades 3, 6, and 9 and science in grade 9. Additionally, schools in Discovery School District were held accountable for student performance on CMEC's (2007, 2008b) assessment regime: OECD's Programme for International Student Assessment (PISA) and the Pan-Canadian Assessment Program (PCAP, formerly known as SAIP), both of which are focused on student achievement in mathematics, reading and writing, and science.

While the focus on testing in Canada has not become high stakes in comparison to the *No Child Left Behind* (U.S. Congress, 2001) program in the USA (Brennan, 2004; Laitsch, 2006; Nichols & Berliner, 2005; Raudenbush, 2004), it has created significant pressure on educators and students as test scores have become the primary public indicator of a student's and a school's level of success, thereby confirming the accuracy of Littky's (2004) contention that "tests ... dictat[e] what we as a society hold valuable in our young people" (p. 5) Holding a view of education that is more focused on personal development, Littky contends that "our addiction to testing is blinding us to what we believe in our hearts are the important lessons our children should learn" (p. 5). Littky's view is shared by Grubb and Oakes (2007), who caution that any gains in test scores most often come "at the expense of other goals ... including equity; curricular relevance; and student interest" (p. 29). Those of us who have been monitoring this phenomenon are beginning to observe the truth in Kohn's (2002) warning that,

> if the sole goal is to raise achievement (in the narrowest sense of that word), then we may end up ignoring other kinds of learning. It's difficult to teach the whole child when you are held accountable only for raising reading and math scores. (p. 20)

As OECD countries pursue an economic globalization agenda, provincial and national boundaries are becoming increasingly blurred. While it is likely that those involved directly in public education (in particular, teachers and school administrators) have thought little about the influence of the OECD's globalization agenda and the concomitant management practice of corporate managerialism on their work, there is little doubt they readily recognize many of the structures, processes, and agendas that are consistent with this management practice and how they impact their daily work (Taylor et al., 1997). These include an emphasis on fiscal efficiency that has resulted in the consolidation of school boards and the creation of larger school districts with fewer staff; school closures; decreased spending on education relative to other public sector spending such as health care that has resulted in crumbling infrastructures, inadequate classroom resources, reduced teacher professional development opportunities; and as noted above, increased accountability of educators and educational leaders for the improvement of student achievement levels on standardized tests.

Consistent with the corporate managerialism agenda, politicians and their officials, irrespective of educational expertise, have assumed the right to make key decisions regarding pedagogical matters in public education and teaching and learning. This has contributed to the displacement of professionally initiated innovation and the erosion of the autonomy of educational leaders and teachers who have been reduced to being mere functionaries who are expected to implement centrally determined curricula (Mulford et al., 2004). "Instead of [educational] organizations having the autonomy to consider, plan, and launch their own change initiatives ..., external forces such as [governments] and ... policymakers, the courts, and various experts have set the change agenda" (Hall & Hord, 2006, p. 1). These externally imposed change agendas appear to be set without any consideration of the fact that professional educators are knowledge workers and leaders who have the professional expertise to lead and make key decisions regarding the organization of schools and student learning.

While school boards have had little input into such externally imposed agendas and have had little control over the consequence of them, they have had frontline responsibility for their implementation and as a result have become primary targets of the public's loss of confidence in the public education system, thereby making them and the entire public education system an easy target for political platforms and even more centralized control by government. Overall, it appears that the impact of globalization and the corporate managerialism agenda has been the entrenchment of political and bureaucratic power-over control of public education by politicians and government bureaucrats—a circumstance that has presented a huge challenge to the sustainability of educational reform.

Challenge 4: A Market-Oriented Approach to School District Restructuring

It is within the above-noted context that over the course of the last two decades, some OECD countries have either eliminated school boards altogether (e.g., New Zealand) or have made them optional (e.g., England) (Anderson, 2003). Within Canada, New Brunswick eliminated school boards entirely in 1996, but reinstated them in 2000 in the form of district education councils (Bowman, 2002). Other Canadian provinces have engaged in school board restructuring that has primarily focused on the consolidation of a number of smaller boards into larger entities. While the long-term impact of school board, consolidation initiatives may be judged as positive (short-term pain for long-term gain), in the short-term, it appears to have negatively impacted the sustainability of meaningful educational reform. At least, this seems to be the case in the home province for Discovery School District. In this province, two major legislated educational restructuring initiatives that occurred over a 15-year period appear to have diverted the attention of educational leaders away from a teaching and learning agenda. The first restructuring in that province was initiated by a Royal Commission Report (Williams, Warren, & Pound-Curtis, 1992) and was legislated in 1997. It resulted in the elimination of a religious-based educational system, the reduction of school districts from 27 Anglophone school districts to 10, and the creation of a Francophone School Board. Discovery School District was created as a result of this restructuring initiative. In 2004, a second restructuring of school districts led to the reduction of the 10 Anglophone districts to four geographically large districts, eliminating all but one of the existing boards, including Discovery School District that had been created only seven years earlier.

During focus group interviews with two individuals who had been superintendents of education during the first period of restructuring, one interviewee observed that his school board trustees felt under siege throughout the 1990s and therefore their attention and that of the educational leaders were diverted from the student learning agenda:

> As superintendent it really took a lot of my focus away from instructional leadership and the normal district leadership activities that I would have been involved in. The whole structure was influenced by the potential of the impending shift.

The second concurred with this view stating that

> During those years, the politics and the demands of that exercise certainly detracted not only my personal energy, but I think the decision making energies of all the senior professional educators in the province as well as the elected school board members . . . . These were very exhausting and very demanding times and I think the system probably suffered . . . from a drift in terms of focusing upon student learning . . . because of that.

Both superintendents concurred that following the actual restructuring event in 1997, the teaching and learning agenda continued to be hijacked because of the requirement to eliminate any duplication of schools that had existed as a consequence of the previously existing denominational system. This process of school consolidation was highly legalistic and mired in political controversy. One superintendent noted that

> the media was consumed with it, and most school closure decisions were challenged in the courts. As a result, there was nothing else that the school board and district personnel, including program specialists, could focus on. Our agenda relating to teaching and learning that we had started earlier was ignored.

Besides, he lamented (with nods of agreement from the other superintendent) that

> the process of school closures that resulted from the 1996 restructuring was primarily focused on questions of finance, the politics of school closures and the legalities of property ownership and the publics' right to be consulted prior to any school closure, thereby distracting us from real educational questions.

In summary, the first restructuring that commenced in the early 1990s refocused the attention of school boards, school personnel, and parents away from issues directly related to student learning toward structural and governance issues. A decade later, schools boards were just beginning to reestablish a focus on teaching and learning when a second restructuring initiative was mandated by government without any advanced notice. Once again the school district focus was on issues of structure as the existing school boards became little more than caretaker boards for several months while the interim boards struggled with their new role.

While the basic school board restructuring event occurred within the designated time frame of five months, the interim school boards and the new district superintendent reported that the newly designed system was underfunded and understaffed and that little meaningful attention could be given to the teaching and learning agenda for the following two to three years. For instance, one superintendent of education commented,

> From an administrative perspective, I will say we made it work, but from an instructional leadership view, I don't think anyone was under any illusion that things were happening in schools the way they normally did .... The ranks of district consultants and program coordinators were decimated!

Moreover, fewer school boards meant that there were fewer school board trustees. As a result, the provincial school boards association struggled with its identity and continued existence for at least two years following the legislated school board consolidation diverting their attention and that of the superintendent away from any consideration of the student learning agenda.

During the 2004 restructuring, Discovery School District was consolidated with three other school districts, which required extensive downsizing of personnel. The superintendent of the newly created district reported that 40% of the district-level support and instructional personnel of the previously existing districts were declared redundant. He noted as well that when this reduction was combined with the elimination of 75% of the trustee positions, this led to the elimination of much of the organizational memory in respect to governance, administration, and instructional development and greatly reduced the possibility of direct engagement of district professionals in the delivery of program support at the school level. The budget allocation for the newly created school district was drastically reduced as well. Review of correspondence between the officials at the Department of Education and the newly formed school district reveals that school district officials contended that it was impossible to provide essential services to schools with the existing resource levels. The typical response from Department of Education officials was that even further reductions were required to realize the savings required by government. The focus was on "making do." Minutes of school board and senior district administrator meetings reveal that during the first two years following this latter school board consolidation, the focus was primarily on policy development and issues related to administrative structures. Additionally, considerable time and attention was given to dealing with and responding to public concerns and media attention related to the poor physical conditions of many school buildings that had resulted from chronic underfunding over the course of several decades. Amidst these challenges, the department of education expected the school board and district administrators to develop an infrastructure plan that would see the elimination of any remaining nonessential schools and to engage in public consultations to fulfill the requirements of government's mandated strategic planning process. Once again, little attention and low priority was given to the student learning agenda.

Both of the government restructuring initiatives as described above reveal that, while governments are able to legislate structural reform, such reform is not necessarily positively related to improvement of student learning, at least in the short term. As a matter of fact, these two reform initiatives described above diverted the attention of district personnel away from a focus on teaching and learning and nullified preexisting district-level reform efforts related to improved classroom instruction. A superintendent summarized the overall impact of both reform efforts as follows:

> While it appears that we may now be poised to offer a better education to our children than in the past, we may have done a disservice to a whole generation of students in the process of getting here as attentions have been diverted away from the core business of k-12 education—student learning.

Several senior district and provincial educators in the province recalled that prior to the first restructuring of school boards, there had been a major focus on the implementation of resource-based learning and cooperative learning that appeared to have gotten lost for more than a decade as school boards and schools dealt with issues of restructuring.

Findings of a recent study of intermediate schooling in that province (Sheppard & Sheppard, 2008) provide some support for the accuracy of the views that there had been little focus on changing teaching practices, as district administrators, program specialists, school principals, and teachers reported that classroom teaching and learning remained largely a teacher-directed phenomenon. For instance, a principal of a large middle school in Discovery School District reported that prior to the 2004 restructuring of school districts, 80% of the classrooms in her school were connected to the Internet, and several classrooms were set up as professional learning centers; however, since then there has been little district emphasis on the integration of technology in the teaching and learning process and the school has not been able to sustain momentum without their support. Another principal reported that,

> the most common teaching strategies ... are chalk and talk. The most common classroom structure is seats and desks in rows ... [and while] all classrooms have three technology drops, there are no computers there. This is not a question of cost because computers can now be purchased inexpensively ($300–$400). But there is not much purpose to put computers in classrooms if teachers are not going to use them.

Beyond the directly observable effects of restructuring on teaching and learning, perhaps little recognized is the extent to which the government-imposed school board restructuring initiatives negate the potential benefits of their own mandated strategic planning process. Prior to being eliminated by government mandate, all school boards in the province had engaged in a lengthy process of strategic planning. For instance, as noted in Chapter 5, Discovery School Board had spent considerable time developing a strategic plan that allowed for the engagement of multiple partners and adaptive learning. Unfortunately, a key partner—the provincial government—was missing from that plan. While the plan could have been adapted to account for major changes from any source, including government, it could not withstand the immediate elimination of the school board itself. Clearly, as a result of government's arbitrary approach to the abolition of the boards, there was considerable loss of time and human and financial resources that had been invested in the strategic planning process by each of the individual boards.

Another casualty of school board consolidation that has been recognized by some is the loss of local leadership capacity when a school board is removed from a region. This is particularly true when school districts have begun to function as professional learning communities and have engaged in various community partnerships in support of both improved student learning opportunities and community development. For instance, Discovery School Board had developed a shared vision that was supportive of student-centered learning. Assuming that previous attempts, a decade earlier, to introduce a student-centered approach to learning had not been successful largely because of challenges related to access to learning resource materials, district leaders proposed that the Internet could provide the solution to the earlier challenges. An impediment to the realization of that proposed solution, however, was that many schools in the district were in geographically rural-remote regions that lacked the necessary technology infrastructure to make this possible. To address this infrastructure challenge, the district brought together various corporate and community partners and was successful in obtaining federal funding for the development of broadband technology infrastructure in those regions. As a result of the leadership of the school district, the entire region gained access to broadband infrastructure.

A former associate superintendent of education observed that Discovery School District had been involved in multiple partnerships of this nature. Referring to a list of Discovery School District Annual Reports (2000–2004), he noted that these partnerships had benefitted not only the school district and its schools, but also other government agencies and the larger community. He opined that much leadership was lost as a result of school board restructuring:

> The government does not see the larger role that a school district can play within a community. The role of the district was similar to the role that teachers played [in previous times] when we had a school in every community—the leadership came from teachers who lived in those communities.... I think in a sense the school board became that individual teacher in the larger community. Because the expertise was in the Discovery School District Office, the skills and knowledge were available everywhere in that district. It provided the leadership that I think we've lost to a large extent.

Given the likelihood that the provision of such leadership at the local level by school boards is a common occurrence rather than an anomaly, if governments were to "wear their systems hat," they would recognize that the consolidation or elimination of school boards may impact more than just the school system. While governments may see the whole, and perhaps even some of the parts, it appears that they do not see the interconnections.

References

Anderson, S. (2003). *The school district role in educational change: A review of the literature.* ICEC working paper #2. Retrieved February 15, 2008 from http://fcis.oise.utoronto.ca/~icec/

Atlantic Evaluation and Research Consultants. (2008). *Intermediate program review.* St. John's, NL: Report prepared for the Department of Education, Government of Newfoundland and Labrador.

Atlantic Institute for Market Studies. (2008). *AIMS 5th annual high school report card (rc5).* Retrieved March 10, 2008 from http://www.aims.ca/.

Bowman, J. (2002). *School boards.* Retrieved August 16, 2008 from http://www.cbc.ca/news/background/education/school_boards.html.

Brennan, R. (2004). *Revolutions and evolutions in current educational testing.* Retrieved February 24, 2008 from http://www.education.uiowa.edu/iae/Pages/IAEoccasional.html.

Brooks, J., & Brooks, M. (1999). *The case for constructivist classrooms.* Alexandria, VA: Association for Supervision and Curriculum Development.

Bryk, A. S., & Schneider, B. (2003). Trust in schools: A core resource for school reform. *Educational Leadership, 60*(6), 40–44.

Canadian Council on Learning. (2007). *State of learning in Canada: No time for complacency.* Retrieved March 10, 2008 from http://www.ccl-cca.ca/.

Conference Board of Canada. (2008). *Employability skills 2000+.* Retrieved March 10, 2008 from http://www.conferenceboard.ca/education/learning-tools/employability-skills.htm.

Council of Atlantic Ministers of Education and Training (CAMET) (n.d.). *English resources.* http://camet-camef.ca/images/eng/library/Publications_English.pdf.

Council of Ministers of Education, Canada (CMEC). (1997). *Pan-Canadian protocol for collaboration on school curriculum.* http://www.cmec.ca/protocol-eng.htm.

Council of Ministers of Education, Canada (CMEC). (2007). *The Pan-Canadian Assessment Program (PCAP) and the School Achievement Indicators Program (SAIP).* Retrieved March 10, 2008 from http://www.cmec.ca/pcap/indexe.stm.

Council of Ministers of Education, Canada (CMEC). (2008a). *Learn Canada 2020.* Retrieved August 15, 2008 from http://www.cmec.ca/2008declaration.en.stm.

Council of Ministers of Education (2008b). *PCAP-13 2007: Report on the assessment of 13-year-olds in reading, mathematics, and science.* Canada: Council of Ministers of Education.

Elmore, R. (2002). *Bridging the gap between standards and achievement: The imperative for professional development in education.* Washington, DC: Albert Shanker Institute.

Emery, E. (2006). *The future of schools: How communities and staff can transform their school districts.* Toronto: Rowman and Littlefield Education.

Fraser Institute. (2008). *Report cards.* Retrieved March 9, 2008 from http://www.fraserinstitute.org/reportcards/schoolperformance/.

Fullan, M. (2005). *Leadership and sustainability.* Thousand Oaks, CA: Corwin.

Galway, G. (2008). Research evidence and educational policymaking: Connecting the polity and the academy. In G. Galway & D. Dibbon (Eds). *Post-confederation educational reform: From rhetoric to reality* (p. 93–110). St. John's NL: Memorial University.

Giles, C., & Hargreaves, A. (2006). The sustainability of innovative schools as learning organizations and professional learning communities during standardized reform. *Educational Administration Quarterly, 42*(1), 124–156.

Goodlad, J. (2001). Convergence. In R. Soder, J. Goodlad, & T. McMannon (Eds.), *Developing democratic character in the young* (pp. 1–25). San Francisco, CA: Jossey-Bass.

Grubb, N., & Oakes, J. (2007). *Restoring value to the high school diploma: The rhetoric and practice of higher standards.* Tempe, AZ: Arizona State University.

Hall, G., & Hord S. (2006). *Implementing change: Patterns, principles, and potholes.* Toronto: Pearson Education.

Hallinger, P., & Heck, R. (1999). Next generation methods in studying leadership and school improvement. In J. Murphy & K.S. Louis (Eds.), *Handbook of research on educational administration* (pp. 141–162). San Francisco, CA. Jossey-Bass.

Hanushek E. (2004). *Some simple analytics of school quality (Working paper no. 10229).* Cambridge, MA: National Bureau of Economic Research.

Hargreaves, A., & Fink, D. (2006). *Sustainable leadership.* San Francisco, CA: Jossey-Bass.

Harris, A., Chapman, C., Muijs, D., Russ, J., & Stoll, L. (2006). Improving schools in challenging contexts: Exploring the possible. *School Effectiveness and School Improvement, 17*(4), 409–424.

Hill, J., & Flynn, K. (2006). *Classroom instruction that works with English language learners.* Alexandria, VA: Association for Supervision and Curriculum Development.

Johnson, G. (2008) Safety vs. freedom. *The Vancouver Sun.* Retrieved May 5, 2008 from http://www.canada.com/vancouversun/index.html.

Knapp, M. (1997). Between systemic reform and the mathematics and science classroom: The dynamics of innovation, implementation, and professional learning. *Review of Educational Research, 67*(2), 227–266.

Kohn, A. (2002). Fighting the tests: A practical guide to rescuing our schools. *Our Schools Our Selves, 11*(3), 85–114.

Laitsch, D. (2006) *Assessment, high stakes, and alternative visions: Appropriate use of the right tools to leverage improvement.* Arizona State University, AZ: Educational Policy Research Unit. Retrieved from http://epsi.asu.edu/epru/documents/EPSL-0611-222-EPRU.pdf

Langdon, B., & Somerton, B. (2007). *Focusing on students: The report of the ISSP and Pathways Commission.* St. John's, NL: Government of Newfoundland and Labrador. Retrieved May 12 from http://www.ed.gov.nl.ca/edu/pub/Focusing_on_Students.pdf

Leithwood, K., Louis, K., Anderson, S., & Wahlstrom, K. (2004). *How leadership influences student learning.* Retrieved Nov. 28, 2005 from the Wallace Foundation Web site: http://www.wallacefoundation.org/WF/KnowledgeCenter/KnowledgeTopics/Education Leadership/HowLeadershipInfluencesStudentLearning.htm

Littky, D. (2004). *The BIG picture: Education is everyone's business.* Alexandria, VA: Association for Supervision and Curriculum Development.

Ma, X. (2002). Bullying in middle school: Individual and school characteristics of victims and offenders. *School Effectiveness and School Improvement, 13*, 63–89.

Mackay, W., & Sutherland, L. (2006). *Teachers and the law.* Toronto: Edmond Montgomery.

Marzano, R., Pickering, D., & Pollock, J (2001). *Classroom instruction that works.* Alexandria, VA: Association for Supervision and Curriculum Development.

References

Mulford, W., Silins, H., & Leithwood, K. (2004). *Educational leadership for organizational learning and improved student outcomes*. Boston, MA: Kluwer.

New Brunswick Department of Education (n.d.). *Atlantic Canada Education Foundation for Essential Graduation Learnings*. Retrieved June 7, 2008 from http://www.gnb.ca/ 0000/publications/curric/acef.html.

Nichols, S., & Berliner, D. (2005). *The inevitable corruption of indicators and educators through high-stakes testing*. Tempe, AZ: Educational Policies Studies Laboratory.

Organization for Economic Co-operation and Development. (2005). Teachers matter: Attracting, developing and retaining effective teachers. Paris: OECD Publishing.

Raudenbush, S. (2004). *Schooling, statistics, and poverty: can we measure school improvement?* Retrieved February 24, 2008 from http://www.ets.org/research/researcher/PIC-ANG9.html.

R. v. A.M. (2008). *Docket: 31496 (SCC 19, April 25, 2008)*. Retrieved July 14, 2008 from http://csc.lexum.umontreal.ca/en/

Sackney, L. (2007). *Systemic reform for sustainability*. Government of Saskatchewan. Retrieved June 25, 2008 from http://www.publications.gov.sk.ca/.

Schlechty, P. (2005). *Creating great schools: Six critical systems at the heart of educational innovation*. San Francisco, CA: Jossey-Bass.

Shaker, P., & Grimmett, P. (2004) Public schools as public good: A question of values. *Education Canada, 44(3)*, 29–31.

Sheppard, B. (1996). Exploring the transformational nature of instructional leadership. *Alberta Journal of Educational Research, 42*, (4), 325–344.

Sheppard, B. (2001, November). *Improving student achievement through teacher professional development*. Paper presented at Canadian Summit on Performance Accountability and Assessment in Education, Toronto, Ontario.

Sheppard, B. (2002. July). *The future of public education in Canada*. Annual General Meeting of the Canadian School Boards Association, St. John's. Newfoundland.

Sheppard, B. (2004, May). *Accountability: Cursing the darkness or shining a light to guide learning?* Paper presented at the Canadian Teachers Federation Annual General Meeting. Ottawa, Ontario.

Sheppard, B., & Sheppard, W. (2008). *Intermediate program review: Background report*. St. John's, NL: Report prepared for the Department of Education, Government of Newfoundland and Labrador.

Shortall, B., & Greene-Fraize, N. (2007). *Education and our future: A road map to innovation and excellence*. St. John's, NL: Government of Newfoundland and Labrador. Retrieved May 12 from http://www.ed.gov.nl.ca/edu/pub/TACReport.pdf

Starratt, R. (2004). *Ethical leadership*. San Francisco, CA: Jossey-Bass.

Stoll, L., & Fink, D. (1996). *Changing our schools*. Philadelphia: Open University Press.

Taylor, S., Rizvi, F., Lingard, B., & Henry, M. (1997). *Educational policy and the politics of change*. New York, NY: RoutledgeFalmer.

Tschannen-Moran, M., & Hoy, W. K. (2000). A multidisciplinary analysis of the nature, meaning, and measurement of trust. *Review of Educational Research, 70(4)*, 547–593.

Ungerleider, C. (2003). *Failing our kids: How we are ruining our public schools*. Toronto, ON: McClelland & Stewart.

U.S. Congress. (2001). No Child Left Behind Act of 2001. Washington D.C. Author. Retrieved August 15, 2008 from http://www.elladvocates.org/documents/legislation_ litigation/No_Child_Left_Behind_Act_of_2001.pdf

Warren, P., Curtis, D., Sheppard, B., Hillier, R., & Roberts, B. (2003). *Facing the challenge: A report of the study group on hours of work*. Department of Education, Newfoundland and Labrador. Retrieved August 15, 2008 from http://www.ed.gov.nl.ca/edu/pub/study/report.pdf.

Western and Northern Canadian Protocol for Collaboration in Basic Education (kindergarten to grade 12) [WNCP] (n.d.). *WNCP Home*. http://www.wncp.ca/

Williams, L., Warren, R., & Pound-Curtis, T. (1992). *Royal Commission of Inquiry into Delivery of Programs and Services in Primary, Elementary, Secondary Education (1992). Our children our future*. St. John's, NL: Government of Newfoundland and Labrador.

Chapter 8
Recognizing What Makes Effective School Districts

Abstract School districts matter, but only effective districts have a positive impact on student learning. After having spent five years researching and working in one school district, the authors outline five understandings related to the complexity of school district leadership and the role of the district superintendent in transforming a district into a professional learning community that positively impacted teaching and learning.

When we started our journey of discovery related to school leadership two decades ago, we were focused on school principals and their role as instructional leaders. After having determined that the effectiveness of instructional leadership was dependent on how it was perceived by teachers and their willingness to engage as leaders, we began to focus on understanding how principals could facilitate the development of a strong teacher leadership team. We believed that if principals and teachers were exposed to the evidence related to shared leadership and school development and if they articulated a commitment to both, change would follow. Much to our disappointment, we learned that our assumptions were not at all accurate. While teacher leadership teams existed in all our study schools, in most they were relegated to being advisory to their school administrators and there was no distribution of leadership roles to other teachers outside the team. Not surprising, then, the majority of teachers in our study schools perceived generally that their engagement in school development was a waste of time. In contrast, in a few higher performing schools, we observed that the teacher leadership team and other teachers felt empowered to make decisions within a defined sphere of influence and viewed decision-making within the school as a shared responsibility.

Similar to many other researchers, we eventually concluded that a huge challenge to the development of teacher leadership was the pervasiveness of the traditional bureaucratic hierarchy and the inability or unwillingness of principals to share power. We pondered, "If we were able to assist schools to develop stronger teacher leadership teams, could these teams be an effective counterbalance to barriers presented by the hierarchy and the negative forces of either the laissez-faire or autocratic school principal?" Once again, it was not long before we realized the fallacy of that assumption. In reality, we found that there exists a great deal of skepticism among formal leaders and followers alike related to any form of collaborative leadership. Most perceive it to be an "ideal" model with little practical application in the "real" world, and even those who subscribe to a collaborative leadership approach find it quite difficult to implement within the deeply entrenched societal mindscapes that are accepting of the norms and practices of the bureaucratic hierarchy.

This led us to conclude that shifting to a collaborative approach to leadership will not occur simply by providing more theoretical information or merely the opportunity, nor will it occur as a consequence of decree. Because collaborative leadership occurs as an interaction of constituents and formal leaders within an always changing context, and because it is outside of existing cultural norms, it will not likely be more than empty rhetoric if not implemented as a complex innovation. This requires commitment and action of a formal leader who functions within, but pushes the boundaries of, constituents' level of tolerance for change. Even then, it will take years to make the transition from reliance on the hierarchical structures and norms of the traditional bureaucracy to a professional learning community where collaborative leadership is the accepted norm.

While our early research work was centered entirely in schools, most of it had occurred in partnership with school districts. As we began to better understand the challenges posed to schools by the school district and the existing mindscapes of the bureaucratic hierarchy, we realized that any fundamental sustainable change toward teacher leadership at the school level was unlikely. Predominantly, school and district structures, policies, regulations, and procedures were designed to maintain order and control, and little attention was given to school development or teacher leadership. District personnel perceived school development as another project that had little bearing on the work of the district or schools. Concomitantly in schools, teachers perceived it as just one of the various perfunctory processes required by the school district.

While there are examples of individual schools led by transformational leaders that have successfully engaged in collaborative leadership and professional learning, these are the exception; even in those schools, sustainability of collaborative leadership and professional learning has been found to be rare when key leaders departed the school. In reality, most schools lack the capacity to lead such a complex transformation. We conclude that without the pressure and support of a school district, most schools will continue to function as isolated bureaucratic hierarchies that are controlled by the school principal—school councils, notwithstanding. In fact, with the frequency of principal succession, school council membership turnover, and the constantly shifting priorities of governments and well-meaning but ineffective school districts, it is more likely that as one school begins to learn, another will unlearn.

Our argument, however, is not that all districts have a positive impact on student learning. As a matter of fact, there is convincing evidence that most school districts, like schools, continue to function as traditional hierarchical bureaucracies that inhibit, rather than facilitate, meaningful school reform. We understand, therefore, the reason some governments have chosen to sidestep school districts altogether and have attempted to reform schools directly through mandates and the use of top-down accountability models. Unfortunately, while such approaches have become popular among politicians in various jurisdictions around the globe because they produce rapid gains in provincial, state, or national test score averages, in the final analysis, the gains are superficial and schools have remained fundamentally unchanged. In truth, learning has become even more superficial and inauthentic, and increasingly large groups of students continue to be disenfranchised.

We conclude that ignoring the potential leadership role of school districts in bringing about meaningful continuous improvement of teaching and learning or eliminating them all together is simply wrongheadedness! The accumulated evidence suggests that all school districts matter. While ineffective districts inhibit school reform, effective districts are a positive force. Neither ignoring the ineffective school districts nor eliminating the effective ones constitutes good practice, however. A more constructive long-term approach is to focus on determining the attributes of effective school districts and strive toward replicating those attributes in all districts. Determining the attributes of effective school districts, however, is not an easy task. Even though there is growing empirical evidence in support of collaborative leadership and professional learning communities as a way forward, it has not found its way into the mainstream practice of either schools or school districts. In sum, there is little precedent and few guidelines available for school districts that desire to lead the fundamental shifts in practices and structural changes required for success.

It was with the objective of contributing to the needed evidence that we engaged in our district study and have written this book. We have spent decades of collective experiences as educational leaders and/or researchers of leadership and have spent five years engaged in research and development, working (as superintendent) and researching (as critical friends), in one school district focused on the facilitation of collaborative leadership and organizational learning. As a result, we have arrived at five understandings or *recognitions*. We are all familiar with the experience of recognition. It means developing insights into a situation or a state that is new for us. Some refer to it as an "aha" moment or eureka. Aristotle referred to it in his *Poetics* as an *anagnorisis*, as a change from ignorance to knowledge (Cave, 1990). In drama, it speaks to the complex actions in the plot where the character acts in ignorance and later realizes (recognizes) what is the truth. For us, at the end of this book, it signifies our new understandings related to the complexity of school district leadership and the role of the district superintendent of education in transforming a district into a professional learning community that successfully leads to meaningful, sustainable educational reform in its schools. These recognitions are as follows:

Recognition 1: *A school district superintendent who has an in-depth understanding of the emerging empirical evidence and developing theories related to educational administration, leadership, and organizational change can facilitate collaborative leadership and organizational learning in a school district.*

Recognition 2: *Leading a shift to collaborative leadership and organizational learning involves considerable risk and is dependent on the existence of mutual respect and trust between constituents and the formal leader.*

Recognition 3: *Structural changes, when combined with clearly defined rules of engagement, facilitate cultural change.*

Recognition 4: *School districts must share a collective moral commitment to each child's learning success and must share a common vision of teaching and learning that will help achieve that commitment.*

Recognition 5: *School district leaders must think systemically and strategically and enlist leaders from multiple sources to collaboratively engage in strategic thinking and adaptive learning.*

Recognitions: Discussion, Implications, and Recommendations

Recognition 1: *A school district superintendent who has an in-depth understanding of the emerging empirical evidence and developing theories related to educational administration, leadership, and organizational change can facilitate collaborative leadership and organizational learning in a school district.*

While there is mounting evidence in support of collaborative leadership and organizational learning as the best hope for bringing about meaningful improvement in organizations such as schools and school districts, the pervasiveness of the bureaucratic hierarchy has shown itself to be highly resistant to such efforts. In truth, shifting from the bureaucratic hierarchy with its multiple control systems is an inherently complex process that requires considerable time and effort and, perhaps more importantly, considerable leadership expertise. Our observations suggest that at the school district level, the superintendent of education is best positioned to lead the required change. If not the superintendent, minimally, it must be led by a senior-level leader in the district, and even then it must be fully supported by the superintendent. In the face of the inherent paradox of encouraging collaborative leadership from within a bureaucratic hierarchy, it is essential that the district superintendent has a strong theoretical base and extensive experience as an educational leader. As noted above, there is no recipe, it is very complex, and it entails considerable risk.

Regrettably, it has been our observation that many school district superintendents do not have the theoretical understanding or experiential base required for success. As a consequence, many superintendents perceive that empirically based approaches of leadership such as collaborative leadership are "out of touch with the real world of practice" and eschew them. These superintendents prefer to focus on management and administrative duties, maintaining the status quo, pandering to the whims of the most vocal school board trustees, and overseeing the implementation of programs that are determined by the government. Perhaps, even more problematic are those superintendents who embrace the concepts of collaborative leadership and organizational learning without sufficient clarity, and as a result, naively ignore the hierarchical realities of schools and school systems. In such cases, the consequences for both the school district and the superintendent are devastating!

Giving attention to improved preparation programs for senior-level educational leaders would most certainly improve leadership practices and over the long run would no doubt contribute to the ever-elusive meaningful educational reforms. Toward that objective, we recommend that researchers and academics must become more concerned about knowledge mobilization and must work directly with senior leadership practitioners to help bring more clarity to the paradoxes of employing collaborative approaches to leadership within the generally accepted bureaucratic hierarchical structures (the real world).

Recognition 2: *Leading a shift to collaborative leadership and organizational learning involves considerable risk and is dependent on the existence of mutual respect and trust between constituents and the formal leader.*

The norms of hierarchical leadership are deeply imbedded into school district cultures and the mindscapes of the major constituents (school board, principals, employees, parents, government officials, the media, labor unions, etc.). For those superintendents who wish to lead change to collaborative leadership, there is a dearth of evidence and lack of a precedent. The journey within the traditional hierarchy is largely uncharted. Consequently, such change is inherently dependent on adaptive learning that is required in order to navigate through the countless minefields that will most certainly be encountered along the way. It involves considerable risk for the leader as he/she must engage as a change agent leading constituents to the very limit of their level of tolerance within their existing mindscapes—a process that is somewhat similar to the ebb and flow of a rising tide—pushing to a new limit each time. While the objective is to challenge the mindscapes, if change goes beyond the limit of tolerance of constituents, the superintendent will lose credibility with them, and the likelihood of success will be limited. As a matter of fact, failure to understand constituents' level of tolerance for change will eventually most likely result in the termination of the superintendent's contract. Accordingly, the superintendent who travels this journey must have a high personal tolerance for risk.

While one aspect of this risk relates to a necessary dependence on adaptive learning that is inherently dependent on tolerance for failure, another aspect is associated with the level of trust that exists between the constituents and the superintendent. This trust is highly dependent on the mutual respect between the parties. On the one hand, if a superintendent is to expect constituents to share leadership, he/she must engage in ethical practices that demonstrate respect for them and their perspectives and that engender their trust. On the other hand, constituents must behave ethically as well, and their practices must demonstrate respect for the superintendent and his/her perspectives.

Success of collaborative leadership is dependent on an assumption that both formal and informal leaders will behave ethically and that most will strive to accomplish goals that have been collaboratively determined. It is, however, particularly risky for the formal leader, given expectations of the traditional hierarchy that he/she is the person in charge and will be held accountable. In actual fact, it is common practice for a formal leader to be dismissed by the corporate board (e.g., school board) when actions of constituents have had serious negative consequences for the organization, even if the formal leader had not endorsed the action in the first place. Consequently, it would be naïve of the superintendent to be unaware of naysayers and saboteurs and those who might be seeking advancement at his/her expense.

While the personal risk for constituents who engage in collaborative processes is not usually as dramatic, it has been well documented that past efforts at shared leadership and shared decision-making have failed because constituents have perceived that they were engaged in superficial and perfunctory processes. Rather than feeling valued for their contributions, they have felt that they were being used as pawns in a game of manipulation. In such circumstances, many constituents who were committed to their leadership responsibilities and had invested considerable time and effort have felt betrayed. Accordingly, many constituents are reluctant to spend time and effort in school or district leadership activities. In schools, teachers have come to believe that their engagement in schoolwide leadership activities takes valuable time from their core work of teaching and learning. Similarly, school principals believe that they have no time to waste on district leadership activities that they perceive are not directly related to their own school.

In order to counteract such negative perceptions of shared leadership, reciprocal accountability mechanisms between formal leaders and constituent leaders must be built into all strategic initiatives in order to engender the mutual trust that is essential to the leadership interaction between constituents and the formal leader. In Discovery School District, the superintendent's articulation of his vision for district leadership as "collaborative and rooted in respect for people" provided the foundation for structural changes (e.g., GACP and GAC) and the development of collaborative processes (e.g., shared decision-making matrices and the new approach to personal professional learning) in Discovery School District. These changes required the active engagement of constituents and formal leaders in collaborative decision making and defined clearly the accountabilities that individuals across the various groups had to one another. For instance, the shared decision-making matrices that were developed collaboratively clearly defined the means through which each group was accountable to the other. The accountabilities of constituents and formal leaders were well defined in the new personal professional development approach as well. As a result of the new approach, teachers were accountable for determining their professional development needs within the context of curriculum and instructional changes necessary to foster student learning in the context of provincial, district, and school policies, goals, and objectives. Formal leaders within the school were accountable for working collaboratively with teachers to determine these priority needs and to work with school district leaders to deliver on those needs. Reciprocally, school district leaders and the school board were accountable for the provision of an adequate level of support to meet the identified professional development needs within the context of the available resources.

Recognition 3: *Structural changes, when combined with clearly defined rules of engagement, facilitate cultural change.*

As noted above, the cultural norms that perpetuate the acceptance of the traditional hierarchy and top-down management approaches are deeply entrenched in the mindscapes of the multiple and varied sources of leadership that define a school district. Entangled with the cultural norms are the hierarchical structures that hold considerable legitimacy because they are the only organizational structures that constituents and formal leaders have ever known. While we agree with others who have observed that structural changes alone will not result in fundamental change, we are convinced that structure and cultural norms are so intertwined that linear approaches that call for initial structural changes followed by efforts at changing professional and organizational cultures will result in disappointment. We propose that changes must be strategically focused at replacing those structures that are supportive of the traditional practices and procedures of the hierarchy with others that support collaborative leadership and shared decision-making. Concurrently, to minimize the possibility that the new structures will not be overwhelmed by the hierarchical norms, the formal leader must ensure that new rules of engagement (e.g., defining shared decision-making) are defined collaboratively by formal leaders and constituents and that these new rules are devoid of hierarchical norms of practice.

In Discovery School District, the structural changes initiated by the superintendent were designed to replace existing district administrative structures that had heretofore supported top-down decision-making. The newly created collaborative decision-making bodies included GACP, GAC, and Families of Schools. In addition to these new groups, the role of program specialists was redefined from a line-authority role (in practice) to a coordinating and boundary-spanning role among schools, within families of schools, and between families of schools and GAC. The structural changes provided the mechanisms for constituents' meaningful engagement in collaborative leadership and contributed to breaking down the cultural norm of teacher isolationism and the collectively held, deeply entrenched, suspicions of collaboration and shared decision-making.

Although the district-level structural changes, noted above, provided the means for shared decision-making, at the beginning the norms of hierarchy continued to predominate decision-making as constituents deferred to those that they recognized had more formal authority within the hierarchy. As a result of this recognition, the superintendent saw the necessity of further defining the rules of engagement. He introduced dialogue and consensus building to GAC members and facilitated sessions through which GAC members could practice in a non-risk environment. Following that, GAC engaged in a lengthy process of developing two decision-making matrices in teaching and learning and repair and maintenance that clearly defined the rules of collaborative engagement.

The initial response of GAC members to the development of decision-making matrices was one of skepticism. As a result of past experience within the hierarchical context, school principals were unconvinced that their input would be given equal weight to district-level personnel. District-level personnel were nervous as well. They were concerned that in a shared decision-making process where principals represented the largest number, their voices would be lost. Both groups were operating within the traditional norms of hierarchy. Principals believed that decisions would be made by those closest to the top of the hierarchy, while program specialists who had always been closer to the top felt threatened. They feared they would lose power, while principals believed that shared decision-making would be merely advisory. These fears and suspicions dissipated as GAC members acquired new knowledge about dialogue and consensus building and as they had opportunities to utilize that knowledge throughout the process of developing the shared decision-making matrices. When the collaborative decision-making matrices were finally developed, each matrix defined the powers and rights of all GAC members in two key areas (teaching and learning and facility repair and maintenance), and thereby contributed considerably to the development of mutual trust among members.

The structural change that led to the creation of GAC provided a forum for collaboration; however, the interventions by the superintendent led to the shared development of rules of engagement for collaborative decision-making. Both the structural change and the new rules of engagement contributed to breaking down the cultural barriers of the traditional hierarchy that previously had stifled constituents' engagement in district-level decision-making. As well, through this process, school principals developed their own leadership capacity, thereby giving them the confidence to distribute leadership in their own schools. While this increased collaborative decision-making in schools, in turn it increased the likelihood that the perspectives brought to GAC by school principals would be derived from collaborative processes at each school, thereby giving school-level personnel meaningful input into both school and district decisions.

Our investigation of the extent to which the collaborative processes employed at the district level were replicated in schools revealed that while few school structures had been altered, teachers had become more engaged as collaborative leaders. We were able to confirm, for example, that teacher engagement in decision-making during the development of the shared vision of teaching and learning was extensive as they engaged with colleagues within their own school and across other schools in their Families. The result of their work was brought to GAC by the principals of each Family, and approval of the shared vision by GAC was based on an assumption that it had been endorsed through a consensus process at each school.

Recognition 4: *School districts must share a collective moral commitment to each child's learning success and must share a common vision of teaching and learning that will help achieve that commitment.*

While it is likely that there will always be differing and completing perspectives of what constitutes student learning, there is little debate that learning is the central purpose of schools and school districts. There is considerable support in the literature, however, for the view that a school district must go beyond a generally understood vague sense of purpose that may exist in a particular province, state, or country

(Deal & Peterson, 1999; Senge, Cambron-McCabe, Lucas, Smith, Dutton, & Kleiner, 2000). As in the advice offered by the Cheshire cat to Alice, in Lewis Carroll's Alice in Wonderland, if you do not know "where you want to get to ... then it doesn't matter which way you go" (p. 57). Given the competing perspectives, it is imperative that a school district develop in collaboration with all its constituents a shared vision of what the purposes should look like in practice, the value assigned to the various aspects of the purpose, how it can be accomplished, and how educational success should be measured.

In spite of the accumulation of supporting evidence, the development of an authentic shared vision (a vision that meaningfully guides the organization and is truly shared) is unlikely to happen without a strong formal leader who is committed to collaborative leadership (Green, 2001; Sheppard & Brown, in press). In some measure this was the case in Discovery School District; however, the story is a little more interesting than that. In actual fact, while the formal leader (the superintendent) had initiated the creation of GAC as a means of facilitating collaborative leadership, it was GAC that instigated the development of a shared vision for teaching and learning as the council members were convinced that it was essential to their goal of improving student learning for each student. Beyond instigating it, they led the process of co-creating the shared vision through the active participation of multiple sources of leadership. As a result of both the development and implementation of the shared vision, the breadth of collaborative leadership expanded as did engagement in organizational learning. It formed the foundation of other initiatives such as the teacher personal professional learning program, and it identified specific roles and responsibilities of district constituents that included parents and school councils. Also, it led to the creation of two classroom practices videos that were used as capacity-building tools for multiple constituents throughout the district.

Recognition 5: *School district leaders must think systemically and strategically and enlist leaders from multiple sources to collaboratively engage in strategic thinking and adaptive learning.*

Glickman, Gordon, and Ross-Gordon (2007) draw our attention to the one-room schoolhouse of the past, where "the teacher was responsible for all that transpired within its four walls; therefore, ... what the teacher wanted to do about the curriculum and instruction was what the school did" (p. 20). The legacy of the one-room schoolhouse has perpetuated norms of isolation and inward thinking in many of our schools today. These norms unfortunately have influenced parents and other community members, and as a consequence, many struggle with how they can be involved meaningfully in schools. Accordingly, systemic thinking and the direct engagement of the larger community in schooling are challenging concepts for those in the teaching profession as well as for other constituents such as support staff, parents, students, and other stakeholders. While some schools within Discovery School District struggled somewhat with engaging the larger community, the district itself appeared to fare reasonably well with the exception of its struggles with provincial government mandates. Discovery School Board and in particular the superintendent was very aware of the role of the multiple factors and varied sources of leadership that impacted on student learning. As a result, the district expended considerable effort to engage all constituent groups in the creation and realization of the district's vision "to challenge and develop the learning and achievement capabilities of each student in a safe, caring, and socially just learning environment." As a matter of fact, the district strategic planning group included representatives of each of the primary constituent groups throughout the school district. However, even this latter group recognized the challenges of engaging other constituents as leaders in support of the district's vision.

The processes and structures that were created to foster collaborative leadership and organizational learning in Discovery School District were created within the context of existing mandated government structures, laws, policies, and regulations. While these government-imposed structures and mandates created challenges for the district in their efforts to bring about systemic reform, they did not prevent it. Even with major government interference, Discovery School District was able to elicit support from other system leaders (e.g., schools councils, school principals, various community and business leaders, the provincial teachers association, and key department of education officials) to moderate the potential limiting effects of some government-imposed initiatives. For instance, it was through working with other system leaders that Discovery School District gained provincial support for its model of professional development. Similarly, the district functioned within the legal mandates of the government-imposed traditional strategic planning model. Even though the government model with its mandated perfunctory processes at times diverted the efforts of the school board and district personnel away from their learning agenda, it did not prevent their engagement in organizational learning. Rather, through collaborative leadership, strategic thinking, and adaptive learning, the district was able to satisfy most of the requirements of the mandated strategic planning process. For Discovery School Board, the official strategic planning document as required by the government mandate was just a snapshot of the board's strategic thinking at a particular point in time as they moved through multiple adaptive learning iterations. Even after major government restructuring that resulted in the elimination of Discovery School Board, the larger commitment to collaborative leadership and organizational learning and some of the processes and structures such as the Families of Schools and the mirror image-plus model for program specialists all survived.

The aforementioned notwithstanding, the elimination of Discovery School Board did compromise the continued development of the growing learning culture as the new board and its much larger school district forged its own identity. Personnel from the previous Discovery School District who held key leadership positions (e.g., the superintendent) in the new district remained committed to sustaining their reform agenda. They advocated for creating the new school district as a professional learning community. Sustainability of that agenda in a new district, where the majority of schools and personnel had little or no experience with it, proved to be overwhelming. In fact, it appears that at least during the first two years many senior-level constituents (e.g., program specialists, senior education officers, assistant superintendents) held a negative perception of those efforts, believing that it was an attempt by those in the previous Discovery School District to impose their structures upon all others. This circumstance was not conducive to the facilitation of organizational learning.

Like Sackney (2007), we conclude that the key to building sustainability of reforms is to build leadership capacity at the multiple levels of the educational system (the classroom, the school and the school district, and the province) and to foster coherence among those levels. In the case of the government-imposed reform that led to the demise of the reform agenda of Discovery School District, the government eliminated a large portion of the leadership capacity that had been developed in that district. Moreover, it set in place policies, procedures, and bureaucratic structures in the form of hierarchical controls in order to ensure accountability and as a means of creating coherence among the various levels within the bureaucracy. Unfortunately, the model adopted was based on the toxic hierarchical assumptions that accountability must be in the form of control and that the "responsibility for coordination and control ... [must be] located at least one level above the people who are doing the work, and learning, or the planning ... where superiors have the right and responsibility to tell subordinates what to do and how to do it" (Duffy, 2004, p. 12). Such a level of central control may give the appearance of improved fiscal and bureaucratic accountability and may force perfunctory compliance of rules and regulations of government; however, for the Discovery School District learning community, the result was that many schools regressed (at least somewhat) to the old restrictive cultural norms that have been identified as inhibiting meaningful educational reform.

Final Thoughts

Our case study reveals that school districts can facilitate collaborative leadership and organizational learning within the context of hierarchical structures, and as a result, they can make a difference to student learning. School districts such as Discovery that function as professional learning communities are adept at working within the complex dynamic interrelated subsystems that define the learning environment for schools. Within that system, school district leaders both influence, and are influenced by, other sources of leadership throughout the entire system. It appears that Discovery School District functioned very well in that environment. District leaders appeared to recognize the complex adaptive nature of the district and the multiple sources of leadership that impacted on student learning. As a result, the district engaged the support of varied leadership partners in initiatives designed to overcome many of the system-imposed challenges to meaningful educational reform that was focused on improved student learning. It was able to deal with government control of financial and human resources, the lack of clearly defined educational purposes, and the impacts of globalization and the increased focus on narrow learning outcomes. Unfortunately, however, it could not withstand a provincial government-mandated school district restructuring that eliminated the district and severely threatened the sustainability of the district initiated reforms.

We are not arguing that school board restructuring is inherently wrong, or even that the elimination of Discovery School Board was ill-advised. Indeed, thinking systemically and in the long term, this decision may have been a correct one. We are convinced, however, that politicians must resist the political temptation of using the promises of educational reform as a convenient political platform, and governments must prevent bureaucrats who know little about teaching and learning from interfering with the work of schools and school boards. We suggest that a more effective strategy for governments is to work with successful school districts and researchers in the field of leadership to ensure that school boards and district leaders are aware of and understand the emerging empirical evidence in support of collaborative leadership and organizational learning and to support them as they engage in the challenging work of transforming themselves from traditional hierarchical bureaucracies to dynamic professional learning communities.

At the outset, we promised that we would give an account of the challenges, mistakes, successes, and self-doubt experienced by one superintendent who attempted to employ his understanding of the emerging empirical literature on leadership to facilitate organizational learning in a traditional school district. We hope that we have been successful in our efforts and that we have contributed to a much needed dialogue about the role of district superintendents in leading meaningful educational reform. There is little doubt that managing the status quo is much easier. The structures and approaches of the status quo are within the generally accepted organizational norms, and leading within that context requires a set of skills that can be learned and applied. For those superintendents who are committed to evidence-based collaborative leadership and the facilitation of a school district as a professional learning community, there are many challenges and few guidelines. We trust that we have left readers with optimism that collaborative leadership can exist within the deeply ensconced societal norms of hierarchy and that we have provided some images of how, with the support of the government and school board, a district superintendent can foster organizational learning directed at improving authentic student learning.

The recognitions that we experienced help us explain what we saw and what we were a part of in this study. They answer questions for us. Yet, we are aware that this is not the final word. Although we recognize certain truths at this time, we are aware that time may change our recognitions! By providing the details we have of Discovery School District, we hope that you will experience your own recognitions. If you can see yourself in this case study, if you too recognize the truths in what we have portrayed, then we have succeeded.

References

Carroll, L. (1951). *Alice in Wonderland and other favorites*. New York: Washington Square Press.
Cave, T. (1990). *Recognitions*. Oxford: Oxford University Press.
Deal, T., & Peterson, K. (1999). *Shaping school culture: The heart of leadership*. San Francisco, CA: Jossey-Bass.

References

Duffy, F. (2004). Navigating whole-district change: Eight principles for moving an organization upward in times of unpredictability. *School Administrator*. Retrieved November 20 4, 2004, from http://www.aasa.org/publications/sa/2004_01/Duffy.htm.

Glickman, C., Gordon, S., & Ross-Gordon, J. (2007). *SuperVision of instructional leadership: A developmental approach*. Needham Heights, MA: Allyn & Bacon.

Green, R. (2001). New paradigms in school relationships: Collaborating to enhance student achievement. *Education, 121*(4), 737.

Sackney, L. (2007). *Systemic reform for sustainability*. Government of Saskatchewan Retrieved June 25, 2008 from http://www.publications.gov.sk.ca/.

Senge, P., Cambron-McCabe, N., Lucas, T,. Smith, B., Dutton, J., & Kleiner, A. (2000). *Schools that learn*. Toronto, Canada: Doubleday.

Sheppard, B, & Brown, J, (in press). Developing and implementing a shared vision at the district level. *International Studies in Educational Administration*.

About the Authors

Bruce Sheppard is a professor in the Faculty of Education, Memorial University of Newfoundland, Canada. He teaches courses in the educational leadership program, including Leadership Theory and Practice and Education Administration Theory and Practice. He has served as Chief Executive Officer/Director of Education in two school boards and has been Associate Dean of Graduate Programmes and Research at the Faculty of Education at Memorial University. His research and publication interests include educational leadership, governance in education, and educational change, all of which are focused on contributing to a better understanding of how to improve authentic learning for each student.

In 2002, Bruce was awarded the Canadian Education Association CEA-Whitworth Award for his contribution to research and scholarship in Canada. In 2003, he was awarded the Educator's Award of Excellence by the Newfoundland and Labrador School Boards Association. Aside from his professional life, Bruce is an avid outdoorsman and a committed family person who values and appreciates his family, his friends, and his rural Newfoundland roots.

Jean Brown is also a professor in the Faculty of Education, Memorial University of Newfoundland, Canada, and teaches courses in the educational leadership program, on Leadership, School Improvement, and Educational Administration. She is currently the Principal Investigator of a large research project, *Building Communities in the New Learning Environment*, funded by the Social Sciences and Humanities Council of Canada (SSHRC) under the program Community-University Research Alliances (CURA). Part of this research is on leadership, with school districts being key partners. On a personal note, Jean is married, with two children and two grandchildren.

David Dibbon is the Dean in the Faculty of Education at Memorial University of Newfoundland where he is also a successful teacher and researcher. His significant and varied research in the areas of organizational learning, leadership and learning, teacher supply and demand, online learning communities, teacher working conditions, teacher education, new teacher transitions, and other policy-related initiatives has contributed greatly to the province as well the broader educational community.

David has just completed a four-year term as Associate Dean of Undergraduate Programmes in the Faculty of Education and has worked in the public school system as a teacher and school administrator; he is currently an elected School Board Trustee with Eastern School District. A strong supporter of public education and the father of two young children, he is committed to research focused on making the school system a better place for students to learn and for teachers to work.

Author Index

A
Achilles, C., 70
Addonizio, M., 29, 36
Anderson, L., 17
Anderson, S., 9, 16, 34, 38, 62, 102, 113
Arguelles, M. E., 37
Argyris, C., 10, 19–20, 28, 50–51

B
Barlow, M., 8
Barnard, C., 2
Barth, R., 1–2, 50, 51, 52
Bass, B., 15–16, 53, 80
Battino, W., 36, 38, 52
Beachum, F., 17
Berends, M., 34, 36, 38, 52
Beresford, C., 37
Bimber, B., 7, 57, 63
Bishop, H., 70
Black, S., 18
Blase, Jo, 16, 17
Blase, Joseph, 16, 17
Bodilly, S., 34, 36, 52, 53
Bogatch, I., 34
Bohm, M., 19
Borko, H., 87
Bossert, S., 15, 18–19
Bowman, J., 113
Brennan, R., 111
Brodt, S. E., 24
Brooks, C., 34
Brooks, J., 110
Brooks, M., 110
Brown, J., 1, 3, 5, 6, 10, 20, 21, 23, 24–25, 51, 64, 71, 93, 95, 98, 129
Bryk, A. S., 16, 23, 63, 108
Burch, P., 21
Burns, J. M., 17

C
Calhoun, E., 93
Cambron-McCabe, N., 129
Carroll, L., 129
Catalanello, R., 69, 83
Cave, T., 123
Chapman, C., 103
Chubb, J., 34
Clem, J., 36, 38, 52
Cohen, J., 5, 64
Conley, S., 35
Corbin, J., 23, 25
Cosner, S., 29, 36, 50
Costa, A., 4
Crandall, D., 12
Curtis, D., 107, 113

D
Datnow, A., 36, 38, 52
Deal, T., 129
Dentith, A., 17
Desimone, L., 87
Diamond, J., 16
Dibbon D., 3, 10, 20, 64, 98
Dibella, A. J., 27
Doyle, D., 34
Doyle, M., 42, 58, 59
Duffy, F., 50, 51, 131
Dufour, R., 10, 11, 18, 51, 72
Duke, K., 15, 17, 19, 55
Dunlap, D., 17–18, 28, 57
Dutton, J., 129

E
Eaker, R., 18, 51
Edmonds, R., 12
Elliott, R., 35, 38, 42, 44
Emery, E., 71, 101–102

Etheridge, C., 50
Evans, R., 62, 93

F
Fink, D., 8, 9–10, 103, 111
Finn, C., 34
Firestone, W., 37, 52
Fisher, R., 41
Fishman, B., 87
Flynn, K., 104
Foster, W., 17
Franklin, C., 5
Freire, P., 19, 49
Fullan, M., 35, 36, 37, 38, 49, 52, 60, 62, 71–72, 82, 86, 102, 104–105

G
Galbraith, J., 56
Gallagher, L., 87
Galway G., 104
Gardner, J., 17, 63
Garet, M., 87, 92–93
Giles, C., 8, 10, 45, 102
Glaser, B., 23, 25
Glickman, C., 9, 18, 85, 86, 87, 93, 129
Goho, J., 70
Goldman, P., 17–18, 28, 57
Goldstein, J., 17, 18
Goodlad, J., 8, 110
Gordon, S., 9, 18, 85, 129
Gould, J. M., 27, 93
Green, R., 7, 36, 50, 129
Greene-Fraize, N., 107–108
Greenwood, D. J., 4, 23
Gregersen, H., 18
Grimmett, P., 9, 111
Grubb, N., 111–112
Guiditus, C., 57–58
Guskey, T., 92–93

H
Hall, G., 9, 10, 11, 12, 15, 16, 28, 52, 54–55, 61–62, 72, 88, 93, 95, 102, 112
Halverson, R., 16–17
Hamel, G., 69, 74
Hansen, J., 57
Hanushek, E., 104
Harris, A., 18–19, 62, 103
Heck, R., 16, 104
Henry, M., 111
Hightower, A., 29, 36, 38, 39
Hill, J., 104
Hillier, R., 107
Hirsh, S., 93

Honig, M., 36, 52
Huberman, M., 23, 25, 36
Hughes, M. T., 36
Hargreaves, A., 8, 10, 45, 62, 93, 102, 111
Hallinger, P., 12, 16–17, 38, 104
Hoy, W. K., 16, 23, 63, 108
Hord, S., 9, 10, 11, 12, 15, 16, 28, 52, 54, 61–62, 72, 88, 93, 95, 102, 112
Hendry, C., 19, 28
Huberman, A., 23, 25

I
Isaacs, W., 19

J
Jantzi, D., 16, 89
Johnson, G., 103
Jordan, C., 5
Joyce, B., 93

K
Kallick, B., 4
Keltner, B., 53
Kirby, S., 34, 36, 52
Kleiner, A., 16, 49, 72, 88, 129
Klingner, J. K., 36
Knapp, M., 29, 36, 101–102, 104
Kohn, A., 9, 103, 112
Korsgaard, M. A., 24
Kouzes, J., 15, 16, 17, 21, 44, 52–53, 58, 63, 80, 97

L
Laitsch, D., 110, 111
Lambert, L., 51, 61
Lampel, J., 69
Lane, R., 70
Langdon, B., 108
Lawler, E., 56
Lazes, P., 23
Leavitt, H., 19, 33, 38, 42, 50
LeCompte, M. D., 4–5
Leithwood, K., 8, 9, 10, 12, 16, 17, 35, 36, 38, 52, 62, 89, 98, 102–104
Leonard, L., 35, 52
Levin, M., 4
Liebeman, A., 85
Lingard, B., 111
Littky, D., 9, 110–111
Little, P., 36
Lord, R., 17, 21, 42
Louis, K.S., 9, 10, 11, 12, 16, 38, 62, 89, 102
Lucas, T., 129

Author Index

M
Ma, X., 103
McCary, C., 12
MacGilchrist, B., 36–37
McHenry, W., 70
Mackay, W., 102
McLaughlin M., 12, 29, 36–38
Macmillan, R., 25
Maguire, P., 38
Mangin, M., 37, 52
Marchand-Martella, N., 3
Marsh, J., 29, 36
Martinez, C., 37, 52
Marzano, R., 104
Meyer, M., 25
Miller, S., 36
Mintzberg, H., 50, 69–71
Miskel, C., 16
Moe, T., 34
Mortimore, P., 36–37
Muijs, D., 103
Mulford, B., 62
Mulford, W., 8, 17, 104
Murphy J., 12, 17–18, 35, 38, 55
Miller, L., 17, 18, 33
Marks, H., 16, 17, 21, 35
Maher, K., 17, 21, 42
Miles, M., 12, 19, 23, 25, 36
Martella, R., 3–5

N
Nelson, R., 3
Nevis, E. C., 27–28, 93
Newton, P., 38, 42
Nichols, S., 111
Northfield, S., 25

O
Oakes, J., 111–112
Ogawa, R., 15, 19
Orlina, E., 16–17
O'Toole, J., 34, 52–53

P
Patton, B., 41
Penuel, W., 87
Peterson, K., 29, 36, 50, 129
Phelps, J., 29, 36
Pickering, D., 104
Pollock, J., 104
Polovsky, T., 37, 52
Popham, J., 9
Porter, A., 87

Posner, B., 15, 16, 17, 21, 44, 52–53, 58, 63, 80, 97
Pound-Curtis, T., 113
Preissle, J., 4–5
Printy, S., 16, 17, 21
Purnell, S., 53

R
Raudenbush, S., 111
Redding, J., 69, 83
Reeves, D., 3, 69, 73–74
Reichardt, R., 53
Riggio, R., 15, 53, 80
Rizvi, F., 111
Roberts, B., 107
Roberts, C., 16, 49, 72, 88
Roberts, N. C., 28
Robertson, H., 8
Ross, R., 49, 72, 88
Ross-Gordon, J., 9, 18, 85, 129
Roza, M., 57
Rusch, E., 34, 35, 50–51
Russ, J., 103
Ryan, J., 85–86

S
Sackney, L., 69, 102, 131
Savage, J., 36–37
Saxl, E., 19
Schön, D., 19–20, 28
Schein, E., 11, 27–28, 49
Schlechty, P., 8–9, 17, 28, 51, 53, 85, 111
Schneider, B., 16, 23, 63, 108
Schuyler, G., 53
Sebring, P. B., 16, 23
Senge, P., 16, 19–20, 27, 28, 49–50, 53, 58, 72, 78, 80, 88, 89, 92, 129
Shaker, P., 9, 111
Sharratt, L., 36, 52
Sheppard, B., 1, 5, 6, 10, 16, 19, 20–21, 23–25, 42, 44, 50–51, 64, 71, 85–86, 89, 92, 95, 98, 104, 106, 107, 115, 129
Shortall, B., 107–108
Silins, H., 8, 17, 62, 104
Smith, B., 16, 49, 72, 88, 129
Smylie, M., 35, 85, 86, 93
Somerton, B., 108
Sparks, D., 17, 18, 19, 51, 93
Sparks, R., 93
Spillane, J., 12, 15, 16, 21, 26, 35
Starratt, R., 8–9, 85, 110–111

Stoll, L., 9–10, 103
Straus, M., 42, 58, 59
Strauss, A., 23, 25
Sutherland, L., 102
Swinnerton, J., 56

T
Talbert, J., 12, 36–38
Taylor, S., 111–112
Teitel, L., 38
Tewel, K. J., 34
Tschannen-Moran, M., 16, 23, 63, 108
Tunison, S., 38, 42

U
Ury, W., 41

V
Vaughn, S., 36

W
Wahlstrom, K., 9, 16, 38, 62, 102
Walberg, H., 9–10
Walker, E. M., 36
Wang, M., 9–10
Warren, P., 107, 113
Webb, K., 70
Weick, K. E., 18
Wenger, E., 56
Werner, J. M., 24
Wheatley, M., 19
Whitener, E. M., 24
Whyte, W. F., 23
Williams, L., 93, 113
Wilson-Jones, L., 70
Woods, P., 21
Wynn, R., 57–58

X
Yamaguchi, R., 87
York-Barr, J., 15, 17, 19, 55

Subject Index

A

Accountability, 8, 17, 19–20, 57, 69, 72, 73, 76, 82, 85, 86, 92, 93, 97, 98, 109–112, 123, 126, 131
Action
   learning, 16, 83, 89
   research, 3–4, 5–6, 23, 90
   researcher, 2, 3, 43
Adaptive learning, 55, 69–83, 101, 102, 116, 124, 125, 129, 130
Administrative council, 7–8, 55–56, 58, 63, 78, 80, 92
Art of inclusion, 20, 49
Assistant superintendent, 1, 4, 7–8, 40–42, 55–56, 62–64, 80, 97, 130–131

B

Back to the basics, 109–110
Barriers, 19, 21, 23, 27, 28, 39, 54, 73, 80, 121–122, 128
Boundary spanners, 56, 61, 78, 98
Brokers, 56, 61
Bureaucracy, 17, 51, 52, 70, 72–73, 122–123, 131, 132
Bureaucratic, 1, 7, 11, 15, 17, 38, 40, 43, 50, 51, 53, 55, 65, 69, 70, 72–73, 83, 86, 101, 107–108, 112, 121–122, 124–125, 131

C

Capacity building, 26, 61, 62, 85–99, 129
Case
   law, 42, 44
   sample, 3
Champions, 26, 49, 54, 56, 61–62, 65, 73, 74, 105
Chief executive officer (CEO), 2, 33, 64
Classroom
   innovation, 28
   practices, 26, 74–75, 78, 86, 90, 94, 98–99, 129
Closed systems, 69, 71
Cognitive frame, 18
Collaborative culture, 16, 55, 60, 69
Collaborative leadership, 20–29, 33–43, 52–57
Complex adaptive organizational system, 70
Complex innovation, 11, 122
Conformity, 19–20
Consensus building, 56, 58, 59, 127, 128
Constituents, 123, 125–131
Conventional planning, 70
"Corridor of beliefs", 21
Credibility, 16, 44, 45, 63, 125
Critical friends, 3, 4, 43–45, 49, 52, 53, 61–63, 74, 78, 80, 81–83, 88, 89, 91, 96–99, 123
Critical mass, 62
Cultural impediments, 18
Cultural norms, 34, 36, 39, 70, 122, 127, 131
Culture of trust, 16, 43, 89

D

Decision-making matrix, 60, 74–75
Developing people, 16
Deviant case sample, 3
Dialogue, 19, 23, 24, 35, 42, 49–51, 53, 55–56, 61, 65, 78, 81, 127, 128, 132
Discovery School District, 5–10, 52–57, 72–77, 88–91, 105–108
Distributed leadership, 15, 16, 19, 23, 26, 89
Double loop learning, 50
Dynamic complexity, 60

E

Economic globalization, 112
Emerging theory, 16
Empowerment, 38, 57, 65

141

E

Engagement, 19, 21, 23, 26, 27, 28, 36, 44, 54, 56, 61, 64–65, 80, 82, 88, 93, 98, 104, 108, 109, 114–115, 116, 121, 124, 126–130
Essential Graduation Learnings, 109
Ethical practices, 125

F

Families of schools, 56, 61–62, 65, 98, 127, 130
Formal leader, 15–29, 123, 125–129

G

General Administrative Council (GAC), 55–65, 74, 78, 80, 92, 94, 126–129
General Administrative Council Planning (GACP) Committee, 56, 58, 126, 127
Governance, 39, 44, 63, 111, 114
Government control, 1, 2, 89, 106–108, 131

H

Hierarchy, 33–45, 50, 52, 53, 73, 80, 121–122, 124–125, 127, 128, 132
High expectations, 16, 19–20, 55, 76, 77, 86, 89
High-stakes testing, 110

I

Implementation framework, 79
Inclusive culture, 16, 55
Individual learning, 16
Informal leader, 15, 26, 125–126
Information and communication technology (ICT), 89–91, 95–96, 98–99, 105
Innovative schools, 6, 24–25, 26, 89
Instructional leadership, 20–21, 50, 104, 113, 114, 121
Interaction, 15, 16–17, 21, 24, 26, 50, 58–62, 67, 95, 104, 122, 126
Isolationism, 9, 18, 101, 127, 129

K

Knowledge mobilization, 125

L

Labor relations, 41
Laissez-faire, 39, 53, 121–122
Leadership
   behaviors, 17, 20, 21, 27
   succession, 5, 25, 122
   team, 22–24, 28, 61–62, 83, 95, 121–122
Learning
   community of schools, 90
   cycles, 71
   school/classroom, 36, 56, 78, 90–91, 138
   school district, 90–91, 131
   village, 90, 91
Legal jurisprudence, 42

M

Major constituents, 44, 125
Managerialism, 112
Media, 2, 44–45, 102, 103, 114, 115, 125
Mental model, 18, 20, 24, 27, 28, 50–52, 58, 61
Mindscapes, 17, 27, 73, 98, 122, 125, 127
Mirror-image, 56, 57, 62
Mirror image-plus, 56, 57, 61–62, 130
Moderately innovative schools, 26

N

National coalitions, 35
Networks, 25, 35–36, 91
No Child Left Behind, 111

O

One best way, 12
On-line Professional Development for Educators Network (OPEN), 91
Organization for Economic Cooperation and Development (OECD), 110–113
Organizational learning, 3–5, 10–12, 15–29, 33–40, 49–52, 55, 123–125, 130–132
Organizational memory, 114–115
Organizational metaphor, 17

P

Paradoxes, 27, 33, 53, 80, 124, 125
Partnership coordinator, 89
Partnerships, 89, 116–117
Perceptions, 3, 6–7, 17, 21, 27, 42, 53, 63–65, 95, 104, 126, 130–131
Personal professional learning, 16, 55, 85, 88, 92–95, 126, 129
Power, 18, 19, 22, 24, 28, 34, 40–41, 50, 53, 57–61, 108, 112, 121, 128
Professional development, 4, 8, 16, 36, 56, 60, 74, 77, 79, 85–99, 112, 126, 130
Professional Development Alliance, 93–94
Professional involvement, 21
Professional learning
   centers, 95, 98–99, 115–116
   community, 2, 11, 17, 28, 38, 49, 50, 52, 55, 73, 81, 121, 122, 123, 130, 132
Program for International Student Assessment (PISA), 6, 111
Program specialist, 3, 39–40, 55–57, 61–62, 82, 92, 98
Public confidence, 8–9

Subject Index

R
Recognitions, 10, 35, 102, 105–106, 109, 123–125, 127–129
Redesigning the organization, 16
Repair and Maintenance Matrix, 58–59, 63, 107, 127, 128

S
School(s)
  Achievement Indicators Program (SAIP), 6, 111
  administrators, 21–22, 107–108, 112, 121, 136
  board, 3–7, 35–38, 41–42, 44–45, 54–55, 58, 62–64, 69, 73–74, 79, 81–83, 91, 93, 95–98, 105–110, 112–117, 124–126, 129, 130, 132
  closures, 6, 44, 112, 114
  consolidation, 2, 6, 42, 44
  councils, 56, 57, 77, 105, 106, 122, 129
  development, 37, 52, 56–57, 71, 74, 83, 85–86, 89, 92, 121–122
  district, 5–12, 15–17, 20, 21, 27, 33–39, 43–45, 49–53, 55, 57, 62–63, 69, 73–75, 77–83, 85, 88–91, 93–98, 103, 105–117, 121–132
  district reform, 106–117
  as troubled organizations, 8–10
Self-doubt, 53–54, 132
Setting direction, 16
Shared decision-making, 50, 56, 57–61, 63, 65, 108, 126–128
Shared images, 27, 54, 73
Shared vision, 16, 19, 37–38, 50, 53–55, 60, 63, 69, 71–72, 74, 75, 77, 78–80, 92, 94–96, 98–99, 116, 128–129
  for teaching and learning, 63, 77, 78–79, 80, 94, 98, 129
Single loop learning, 50
Site-based management, 37, 63, 65
Socioeconomic status, 10, 103, 105–106
Static schools, 26
Strategic planning, 37, 54–55, 69–74, 82–83, 115–116, 130
Strategic thinking, 55, 69–83, 124, 129–130

Structural impediments, 18, 61–63, 73, 114–115
Student
  and family background, 103
  focused, 16, 54, 92
  learning, 1–2, 6, 9, 10–12, 16, 19, 33, 40, 73–74, 77, 79–82, 85, 93–95, 97–99, 101–104, 106, 112–116, 121–123, 126, 128–132
Superintendent, 1–5, 7–8, 12, 15, 38–45, 49, 51–65, 69, 72–74, 80–83, 88, 91, 92, 97, 106, 113–116, 121, 123–132
Sustainability, 25, 83, 91, 101–117, 122, 130–131
Systemic reform, 104–105, 130
Systems
  challenges, 83, 101–117
  thinking, 16, 54, 105–106

T
Teacher(s)
  commitment, 86
  perceptions, 3, 6–7, 64–65, 95
Teaching and learning, 5, 16, 25–26, 28, 37–38, 55–61, 63, 74, 75–80, 92, 94–99, 107–108, 112–116, 121, 123, 124, 126–129, 132
Teaching and Learning Matrix, 59–60, 63
Teamwork, 38
Theoretician, 12
Tolerance, 43, 52–53, 63, 97, 122, 125
Top-down models, 22, 39, 42
Transformational leadership, 21
Trends in Mathematics and Science Achievement (TIMSS), 6
Trust, 16, 19, 23–25, 27, 41, 43–44, 54, 59, 63, 89, 108, 123, 125–126, 128, 132

U
Undiscussables, 28
Union officials, 41
Unlearning, 18–19, 20, 53

V
Vertical system of authority, 17–18, 22